LIKE LOVE

MACHETE

Joy Castro, Series Editor

LIKE LOVE

Michele Morano

MAD CREEK BOOKS, AN IMPRINT OF
THE OHIO STATE UNIVERSITY PRESS
COLUMBUS

Library of Congress Cataloging-in-Publication Data

Names: Morano, Michele, author.

Title: Like love / Michele Morano.

Other titles: Machete.

Description: Columbus : Mad Creek Books, an imprint of The Ohio State University Press, [2020] | Series: Machete | Summary: "A personal essay collection about unconsummated romance in all its forms. The author discusses unconsummated romance and her relationships with partners, parents, strangers, and friends"—Provided by publisher.

Identifiers: LCCN 2020005794 | ISBN 9780814255988 (paperback) | ISBN 0814255981 (paperback) | ISBN 9780814278192 (ebook) | ISBN 0814278191 (ebook)

Subjects: LCSH: Morano, Michele. | Love—Miscellanea. | Interpersonal relations. | American essays—21st century.

Classification: LCC PS3613.O71575 A6 2020 | DDC 814/.6—dc23

LC record available at https://lccn.loc.gov/2020005794

Cover design by Nathan Putens

Text design by Juliet Williams

Type set in Adobe Palatino

♾ The paper used in this publication meets the minimum requirements of the American National Standard for Information Sciences—Permanence of Paper for Printed Library Materials. ANSI Z39.48-1992.

"To love or have loved, that is enough. Ask nothing further. There is no other pearl to be found in the dark folds of life."

—Victor Hugo, *Les Misérables*

Unconsummated: adj. (from the Latin *consummatus*):
1. regarding marriage or a relationship: without sexual union
2. regarding organic matter: not decomposed
3. regarding everything else: imperfect, incomplete, unfinished

AUTHOR'S NOTE

This is a work of truth more than fact. While the events that follow are accurate to the best of my memory, other people will remember things differently, and I've made no effort to account for that. I have, however, altered identifying details to preserve the privacy of some people whose good or bad fortune led their lives to intersect with mine.

CONTENTS

THE LAW OF DEFINITE PROPORTIONS

In the 1990s, many of the single, thirty-something women I knew found themselves involved with men who, we joked with some bitterness, did not put out. One friend, Emily, bemoaned her fake boyfriend who talked to his long-distance fiancée every night and, in between, spent most of his free time with Em. He'd call before running to Walmart then pick her up on the way, needing advice, he said, about the bookcase he wanted to buy. Light wood or dark wood? "No wood is all I'm getting," she lamented over tumblers of wine.

Rachel got a little further, though her guy often preferred to sleep when he slept over. There were rumors around town about where he spent other nights, rumors that, true or false, might not have mattered if he'd been more attentive to her. "Why does he come to my house just to cuddle?" she complained. "Who am I supposed to be, his mother?"

I held out the longest, silently judging my friends for taking up with men who received more than they gave.

"You deserve better," was my mantra, and Emily or Rachel or Carolyn or Jill would counter that in the various college towns where we were graduate students, with a large segment of the population under twenty-one and most of the straight men our age married, what were we supposed to do? Where was a single, sane, smart-but-not-too-nerdy grown-up to be found?

Just down the hall from my summer classroom came the answer one year. While I taught a literature course, he led a study session of chemistry for non-majors. We said hello on the way to class, his smile pulling me in like a warm embrace, and the combination of shoulder-length blond hair and dark eyes reminded me of a grade-school crush. When he introduced himself, I blurted out that he didn't seem like a scientist. He seemed too cool, too grounded. "Are you sure you're not a historian?" I asked, and he threw his head back, laughing. Within a week, he was sleeping in my bed every night.

Understand what I mean to say: within a week, he was *sleeping* in my bed every night. Sharing a pillow. Spooning me from behind, one arm draped over my waist. Snoring.

Now, all these years later, it seems a form of madness, like the scene in M. F. K. Fisher's *Long Ago in France,* when a young man, a boarder in the same house where Fisher and her new husband live in Dijon, wakes her late at night to ask for help. In his room, she finds a young woman lying naked on his bed in a state of what appears to be nervous collapse. From the tray of empty dishes on a side table and the crumbs strewn across the woman's belly, Fisher concludes that the man has used her body like a table, eating a full meal from it without accepting any of what she offered. Fisher sends the man away and tends to the woman, wiping her skin with alcohol and cool cloths, covering her with a blanket, returning her slowly to the disappointing world. The disdain Fisher feels toward the young man fairly leaps off the page.

As it should, I thought when I first read this passage. And yet before long there I was, not entirely naked and not in a paralyzing state of sexual arousal, but wanting. All the time, wanting.

He had a girlfriend, he explained the first time he came by, guitar in hand after I told him I'd recently bought one and was trying to learn the basics from a book. We sat on my living room rug for a couple hours, facing each other cross-legged, my two cats sprawled between us. While I strummed simple chords, he played a Spanish-sounding piece he'd written himself, right hand picking so delicately it made me squirm. I noted the way his long arms held the guitar, the way his chest curved over the instrument, concentrated and relaxed, the way his smile seemed to contain a hint of surprise.

The girlfriend lived halfway across the country, as did he. He'd been a graduate student at my Midwestern university before transferring to a more exclusive school out east, but he'd been working with an advisor on a grant project when he left and was back for the summer to continue that research. I remarked that it must be hard to be away from his girlfriend for a couple of months, and he said not really, since they'd always lived in different states and were used to the distance. Eventually he described their relationship in more detail, how they'd bonded over a similar, conservative privilege that somehow bred open-mindedness in each of them, and how, despite her liberal beliefs, she was committed to remaining a virgin until marriage.

"Why?" I gasped, as though he'd confessed to believing in unicorns. As he explained the traditions of her religion and family, I gave myself a silent talking-to. He was seven years younger than me—too young. There was no reason to get mixed up in this next half-generation, with its aversion to healthy sex, its retro-fetishizing of virginity. Why bother with a guy who gave every indication of interest in me while remaining loyal to a celibate girlfriend a thousand miles away? "You deserve better," I told myself.

But somehow, the scientist and I ended up taking long walks through town and listening to music he thought I'd like, and late one night, after a guitar lesson followed by a few beers, he went from sitting on my bed in front of the stereo to leaning back, eyes closed. "I'm too tired to walk home," he said. "Maybe I'll just stay here tonight." He slept in his shorts and tee-shirt, as did I, the two of us politely sharing my narrow bed. The next night he stripped to boxers and I changed into a sleep shirt, and if this were a work of fiction, no one would believe it. For six weeks we slept together every night, romantically but chastely, in a parody of everything I understood about how relationships go.

Romantic friendship has always existed. In the sixteenth century, Michel de Montaigne described the instant chemistry of meeting soul mate Etienne de la Boetie: "we found our selves so surprized, so knowne, so acquainted, and so combinedly bound together, that from thence forward, nothing was so neer unto us as one unto another." In the nineteenth century, Emily Dickinson wrote exuberant love letters to her sister-in-law Susan Gilbert, in which she sent "shy," secretive kisses and cooed, "If you were here—and Oh that you were, my Susie, we need not talk at all, our eyes would whisper for us, and your hand fast in mine, we would not ask for language . . ."

The term "romantic friendship" tends to describe male-male or female-female bonds in the time before, as Margaret Atwood writes, "Freudianism swept through same-sex relationships like the plague." After that, intimacy became sexualized, suspect. Of course many romantic friends were what we would now term gay couples, but others seem to have enjoyed a closeness that might include kissing, cuddling, sharing beds and even homes outside the realm of sexual connection.

I understood that kind of friendship, having had best girlfriends growing up, but nothing approaching a romantic friendship with a man had seemed possible before that summer. The idea of sleeping beside an attractive, charming guy whose off-limits status only enhanced his appeal would have been ludicrous even the day before our arrangement began. Only Gandhi had that kind of restraint, if you believe he didn't actually touch the naked young beauties he slept beside to test his celibacy. A week into our arrangement, though, once I got over my own disbelief and more or less accepted the sexual boundary between us, something shifted and an electrified intimacy took over.

When I woke in the morning, curled onto my side at the edge of the bed and blinking back to reality, it took a moment to remember the context. The room was silent except for a car engine asserting itself outside, and when that fell away I heard his breath, felt the warmth of his back against mine. I shifted a little, stretching my legs and rolling over to look at the ceiling, and he responded by turning toward me with a smile. "Good morning," he said. "Hey," I replied, closing my eyes to allow the conversation to begin. We talked about strange dreams and stranger memories and what lay ahead that day, and soon one or both of us got up, the spell broken, and the longing began. Already I wanted that time back, that quiet, mumbling, sweet, if not wholly innocent, connection.

Often I came home to his voice on the answering machine, its soft, enticing inflections, its invitation making my lower abdomen clench. I'd play the message two or three times, smiling at the texture of his words, "want" and "maybe" and "later." Once after I cancelled class to hold student conferences in my office, I arrived home to a long message of trembling guitar strings. The melody toggled between serious and playful, the spun steel lamenting and laughing and occasionally squeaking under the soft calluses of his fingertips. He missed me, the music conveyed, and hoped I missed him, too.

We weren't lovers. But we weren't *not* lovers either, more like the parties in romantic friendships conducted so often through letters. Bodiless. Transcending ourselves. Existing for a little while in purely idea form.

The scientist still had friends in town, one of whom was dating a friend of mine. During the sociable summertime we were each invited to the same backyard barbeque and to the Fourth of July fireworks show a couple towns over and to a good-bye dinner for another grad student who'd had enough of academia and was off to seek her fortune as a screenwriter. We spent these evenings mingling separately, catching each other's eyes across a room or a yard or making charged small talk beside a beer cooler. Often we left separately and met up back at my place, yawning and ready to turn out the light and talk. We couldn't get enough of talking, mostly about things that were personal only in a metaphoric sense. I summarized the story or play or novel I was preparing to teach, and we puzzled out the motivations of one character, the desires of another. He told me about the laws of chemistry his students had to remember, like the First Law of Thermodynamics, which says that the amount of energy in the universe is finite, or the Law of Definite Proportions, which says that the parts of a chemical compound always appear in fixed ratio: every drop of water in the world contains two molecules of hydrogen and one of oxygen. That law seems obvious now but wasn't always so, and lying in the dark, side-by-side or one behind the other, we mused about what would seem obvious in a couple hundred years, talking until our voices began to fade, until longer pauses appeared between words, until I said, "Goodnight" and he said, "Have a good sleep," and we slipped into dreamscapes lined with metaphor.

By the end of a month, I was in love with him. Fully, blindingly in love, with an intensity that defied logic and may not have happened so profoundly without the attention we paid only to words night after night. I began to understand how the no-sex-before-marriage edict might deepen feelings of love and, at least in theory, carry a couple over the threshold into marriage. Not that I wanted anything like celibacy in my life. But here it was, a curious thing to behold.

Emily Dickinson felt tortured not by her friend Susan's marriage to her brother but by physical distance. "I need you more and more," she wrote in 1852, "and the great world grows wider, and dear ones fewer and fewer, every day that you stay away—I miss my biggest heart; my own goes wandering round, and calls for Susie." Her letters swell with the painful pleasure of separating and coming together again.

But at least she had reunions to look forward to, I thought that summer. In my case a permanent separation loomed. As the days ticked by and the prospect of his leaving neared, our interactions became layered with future loss until, in the middle of one night, I woke to his hand gently rubbing my stomach. The circles started small, just above my navel, and slowly grew, his touch warm even through my tee-shirt. I lay still, eyes closed, knowing that he was giving in to the impending sadness, reaching out to stave it off, and I had only to turn toward him to change the parameters of what we were up to. But as much as I wanted to do that—*really* wanted to do that—I resented this clandestine seduction. Come daybreak, we might both act as if nothing had happened, relegating our union to the cover of night, and that seemed even less bearable than the way things had been so far. I decided to go to the bathroom and, upon returning, to ask his intentions and hash this out and then, I hoped, get down to business. But when I came back to bed, he was fast asleep.

The next afternoon I ended my class early and was already home when the phone rang. "I looked for you," he said in that soft, strong voice. "Everything OK?"

Everything was not OK. What was this insanity? Why was he sleeping, *sleeping* with me every night? How dare he treat me this way!

Within minutes, he was at my door. He hadn't woken up at all, he said, and didn't remember rubbing my stomach. He apologized and talked about his girlfriend, twenty-four years old and living with her parents while figuring out how to shape her life. She was a brilliant woman he'd once loved deeply, and although the relationship probably wasn't going to last, he felt he owed it to them both to spend some time with her before deciding. In the meantime, well, he hadn't expected to meet someone like me. He apologized again but also insisted he wasn't sorry for spending so much time with me.

I rolled my eyes, huffed and puffed, called him a cliché. I also calmed down, and after a while we managed to laugh. Well, I thought, now I understand how this sort of thing happens. As so many of my friends had already learned, it's hard to turn down a smart, attractive, devastatingly articulate man who makes you feel important, desired, something like loved. When bedtime rolled around, there he was again.

Self-respect is a curious beast. When I was young, nineteen or twenty, my boyfriend invited me to dinner at a very nice restaurant. We agreed to meet at his house, where I often spent Friday nights. No one was home when I arrived, so I sat on the front steps, watching cars come down the road, waiting. This went on for over an hour. I thought about leaving, but it was unlike him to be so late, and besides, I lived half an hour away. If I left, there'd be no coming back that night, and I was feeling not just hungry but amorous.

Eventually his roommate's car pulled into the driveway and they both got out. They often drove to work together, and on this day the roommate had accepted an invitation to stop by a co-worker's barbeque on the way home. My boyfriend was riding with him, so of course he stopped, too, what else could he do? But here's the thing: the co-worker lived a quarter mile away, her house nearly visible from the steps where I sat waiting. He could have walked from there. He could have come to get me. He could have declined the pulled pork and coleslaw.

In the list of life's regrets, this one ranks surprisingly high, even decades later. I still wish I'd left as soon as he offered an explanation. I wish I'd said, nope, sorry, I deserve better, because doing so would have kept me on good terms with self-respect. But at nineteen or twenty it's hard to know your own worth, even harder to imagine that there will be other men who will love you, some of them in the way you want to be loved. So I let him take me to dinner, where he nursed a beer because he was too full to eat anything more, while I picked at sea scallops and tried to imagine how our story would turn out.

That long-ago evening was on my mind a couple weeks after the scientist moved back east. I was having dinner with a male friend who must have noticed how my fingers kept circling a sore spot in the center of my chest, self-soothing, though I tried to make it seem like a casual gesture. My friend, who knew the scientist a little bit and knew me better and had an inkling that we'd spent a lot of time together, asked point blank what was going on, and I told him, rubbing my chest the whole while. The tale ended with, "I know it's a ridiculous situation, but I kind of admire him for not cheating on his girlfriend."

Well. My friend's eyebrows shot up, and he glared for a moment before setting me straight. If I thought for one minute that the scientist hadn't been cheating all summer, I was crazy. Anything, *anything* he withheld from the girlfriend was a betrayal.

Because I knew that this friend had started sleeping with his current girlfriend before breaking up with the previous one, and not in the chaste way I had going on, his words meant something. He ought to know about betrayal, I thought, stabbing at my refried beans, transported by the bitter taste in my mouth to that fancy restaurant a dozen years before. The difference this time was that I didn't have the option of breaking up with a guy who'd treated me badly because there was no relationship to end.

Or was there? The scientist had called me almost every day since he left, going silent only while visiting the girl-friend, during which time they decided to give themselves one last chance. In the week since he reported that news, I realized how confidently I'd been narrating the story to myself with a different ending: my reward for the summer's patience was supposed to be that he'd break up with her and promptly declare his love for me. That was the happy outcome my patience had earned. When the opposite happened, I chastised myself. I should have seen it coming. It was my fault for slipping into bed with him each night, for doing exactly what I'd counseled friends against, only more so. I deserved every bit of the sadness coursing through my veins.

But after my male friend set me straight the way no female friend could have, another option appeared, one that transformed disappointment into action. I could refuse to be treated this way. Even if I'd been a willing participant in this affair, I had every right to be angry, and it wasn't too late for self-respect. When I got home, I phoned the scientist and left a message that trembled with emotion. "If you think you weren't cheating this whole summer, you're crazy," I announced. "Anything, *anything* you withhold from your girlfriend is a form of betrayal." I ended by telling him not to call me again.

Of course he called as soon as he got the message, and I told him off, listened to his apologies, then told him off again. After that we didn't speak for many months. Eventually he did break up with the girlfriend and did call and did come back for another summer, but it's not that story that haunts me now. It's that first summer, that bizarre six weeks, that still puzzles.

The law of definite proportions says that H_2O is water at the top of the glass and in the middle and down below, and if one hydrogen molecule lets go, what remains is no longer water. This is true and incontrovertible. Love is not water, of course, not defined by chemical bonds or governed by any laws science has discovered. But maybe some forms of love behave like chemical compounds, taking hold in a permanent way, regardless of situation or time, and maybe unconsummated romance, with its dance of desire, its perpetual hope for the impossible, makes the bonds adhere more strongly.

All these years later, I sometimes dream of the scientist and the emotions of that summer, and in the morning I wake so disoriented it takes a few minutes of blinking into reality, of recognizing the blue-gray walls and the soft breaths of the man beside me to know who I am. Frame by frame I go over the dream, as if pressing my tongue against a sore tooth, drawn to the pressure and release, the pull and relief. And then it's gone, real life resumes, my day is filled with work and play, with laughter and frustration and joy and love, and the past recedes until, in the dark of an unpredictable night, it returns once again, real yet not real, over yet incomplete, ripe with exquisite longing.

BREAKING AND ENTERING

There is nothing illegal about breaking into your own home. As long as your name is on the deed, it doesn't matter if your worn silver key won't unlock the back door. It's still your house, so go ahead: smash the window and let yourself in.

That's what my mother's lawyer had advised, and it's what she intended to do.

The rest of us waited while she rummaged through the garage. It was 6:00 on a late September evening in New York's Mid-Hudson Valley, the air soft and warm, maple helicopters twirling into the gravel driveway. My brother and I stood in the small backyard and looked at the shingled houses to the side and behind us. A month before, we'd jumped rope on that patio, swum in that above-ground pool, sauntered up these back stairs toward a jar of sugar cookies. It was the end of summer vacation then.

Now my mother emerged from the garage carrying a brick. "This'll work," she said, holding it against her shoulder as she climbed the back steps.

Uncle Marty, recently married to my mother's sister, held the screen door open, while three grown cousins stood in the driveway. It was absolutely illegal for any of them to break the window, so they kept their distance and called out encouragement.

"Use the end of the brick," Andy advised.

"Be careful you don't put your hand through," added Philip.

After the first try, Timmy said, "Harder, Aunt Reet," and my mother nodded. She'd never broken a window before.

That year, my parents' arguments had focused on the usual topics—money, respect, the ugly dining room table one of them wanted to replace and the other wanted to keep—and also, increasingly, on the new friends my mother made after taking a part-time job at the printing factory where my father was a supervisor. She worked early in the morning and was home by noon, while he went in at 2 p.m., an hour before the shift change that released my mother's full-time co-workers for the day. Sometimes those co-workers stopped at our house on their way home, coming in for glasses of soda or iced tea, and it troubled my father that employees he oversaw were in his home when he wasn't there.

"I don't want people thinking I treat them different because they're your friends," he explained.

"So don't treat them different," my mother responded.

A couple times a week, a woman named Jan stopped in, chatting with my mother at the kitchen table for half an hour before continuing home. Soon she began returning in the evening with her family: a curly-haired boy with dimples who was twelve to my eleven; a blonde girl of ten to my brother's nine; and a preschooler with eyes so large and lashes so long he didn't seem real. And there was Maggie: a tall, thin woman dressed the way Jan dressed, in jeans and tee-shirts, the mannish outline of a wallet in her back pocket. Maggie always brought her guitar, and when we kids tired of playing flashlight tag, we gathered in a circle on the living room carpet around her. Maggie strummed and we harmonized as best we could to "This Land Is Your Land," "Take Me Home, Country Roads," "Blowin' in the Wind," a set that felt both corny and electrifying. It was 1976, the year of the bicentennial, when the values of freedom and independence loomed large, even as rumors floated through a printing plant in Poughkeepsie, New York, about the supervisor's wife and her new friends.

One day a few months before we broke into the house, while my mother and I were running Saturday morning errands, she complained about how unreasonable my father was being. "He can't control my life," she said, one hand on the steering wheel and another bringing a cigarette to her lips for a long drag. "They're *my* friends. He's just jealous."

I looked at the gray sky, wondering if the rain would hold long enough for a bike ride down our street to the hill where trees fell away and a mountain across the Hudson River shone blue or purple, depending on the weather. Farther to the north was Albany, and to the south the mythical New York City, where everything worthwhile originated. I liked looking at the view and imagining a life extending far beyond familiar territory.

"Honey," my mother said casually, as if she, too, were thinking about the weather, "do you know what the word 'queer' means?"

As an adolescent determined not to admit ignorance about anything, I scrolled through memory, through playground interactions and whispered conversations about taboo subjects, searching for a clue. But although we kids threw the word "queer" around in the same tone as "douchebag" and "peckerhead" and "prick," the only synonym I could think of was "weird."

My mother explained the alternate meaning, while I gazed into the clouds and felt the earth spin faster on its axis. Men and men? Women and women? In the back of my closet at home were three Barbies and one Ken doll, and in all those years of creating dramatic storylines between them, I hadn't once thought to pair up the girls. Why not? How could imagination have failed me so completely? And what other truths, I wondered, were staring me right in the face?

My mother described the attitudes of people at work about Jan and Maggie, how they gossiped and acted so high and mighty. "Why should they care about other people's private lives?" she asked, before adding, "And anyway, Jan and Maggie aren't queer."

I didn't respond, thinking of how much stricter Maggie was with the kids than Jan was, and how they checked in with each other about plans and sometimes winked when they thought no one was looking. My mother was missing something obvious, but I didn't tell her so. Instead, I settled into the new knowledge of their relationship with a sense of optimism. My mother, who resembled Lucy Ricardo with her slim figure and 1950s-style dresses, had always been old-fashioned, but her attitude about Jan and Maggie made her seem hip and open-minded, less like June Cleaver than Shirley Partridge, the mother I'd always wanted.

A couple months later, on a hot summer afternoon when Jan was visiting, I walked into the kitchen to ask my mother a question. She stood in front of the refrigerator, back leaning against it as Jan grasped her arms and leaned forward. My mother made as if to turn her head away, but Jan was too quick, and as their lips touched, I stood frozen. In the moment before they noticed me, my mother recovered her balance, closed her eyes, and leaned forward, the surprise on her face melting into pleasure.

The sound of shattering glass startled us all. "Stay here," my mother commanded, once she'd reached through the window and unlocked the door. No one moved until she located the broom and dustpan and cleaned up the mess. Skipper, the auburn mutt we'd left behind, was barking himself frothy in the cellar, and once we all stepped inside and closed the back door, my mother let him out. Skipper leapt into her arms, howling and licking her face, his long body spinning in circles as grief and gratitude rippled under his matted coat. "OK honey, stop. OK," my mother said, leading him outside and tying his leash to the clothesline.

Back inside, she told everyone to hurry. The aim was to get as much as we could before one of the neighbors called the police or, worse, my father.

I walked from the newly remodeled kitchen through the dining room and into the living room, where everything seemed both familiar and strange. I couldn't help pausing before an end table to examine last year's school pictures, then sat in an armchair and gazed toward the television. Had there always been this much space? And had we really, just a month before, belonged here? My mother and brother rushed upstairs, while two of the cousins hoisted the couch and Uncle Marty pulled knickknacks off the stereo cabinet. There was the mug painted with a map of Lake George, the bobblehead of Thurman Munson, the uncracked copy of James Baldwin's *Go Tell It on the Mountain* that had come home in a box of books from the plant. I could have drawn every inch of the room from memory.

"Go get your stuff, girl," cousin Timmy said. He was a handsome seventeen-year-old and said "girl" with the same teasing affection he used with his sisters, so I went upstairs, eager to see my room. In the cramped house where we'd been staying, my clothes stored in a small duffel bag, I felt unmoored. Everything was strange, including the bus to middle school and the routines that enabled eight people to share a bathroom. Three kids slept in one bedroom, two slept on the sectional sofa in the living room, and all three of the women shared a double bed, with Jan positioned in the middle between my mother and Maggie, who seemed to suspect but not really to know that my mother and Jan had fallen in love. In my presence, when the other kids weren't around, my mother and Jan talked openly about wanting Maggie to move out, but the house, a small duplex in the country, was owned by her parents. "We just have to be patient," they kept saying. The new apartment my mother had rented was part of a larger plan, although she hadn't explained, and didn't really seem to know, how it was all going to work out.

I climbed the stairs, the second and fourth steps creaking as they always had, the landing bright with western sun. How small the hallway seemed now, with four doors radiating off it. How narrow my parents' bedroom and how dim my own, facing east in the evening light. "Hurry," my mother said, stepping out of Michael's room with a bulging black garbage bag in her hand and rushing downstairs again.

When my mother first told me about the plan to break into our house, I thought it seemed fair, right, reasonable.

I owned things, after all, things that belonged to me, and I wanted them. Besides, now that we were moving into our own place, we needed beds, a couch, pots and pans, towels. And I needed—more than clothes or furniture or even food at this point—my record albums and magazines and the posters taped to my bedroom walls.

The Bay City Rollers had come into my life the previous winter in what felt like divine intervention. Late one Saturday afternoon, I was flipping through TV channels, past a Three Stooges movie and professional bowling, when a circus-like concert appeared on the screen. There was a round stage, a studio audience, balloons and confetti raining down around a band that seemed wonderfully foreign. They wore eager smiles and wild clothing—plaid-trimmed jackets and short pants with striped socks and sneakers—and seemed earnest in a way that was almost embarrassing. The audience heaved with girls wearing similar uniforms and waving plaid scarves overhead, their faces contorted in shrieks. Now and then one of them broke through the security barrier, catching the lead singer in a headlock or pulling a guitarist to the floor, making my brother howl with laughter. I'd seen footage of hysterical fans at the Beatles' concerts but hadn't known something like this was possible, not with the stripes and plaids and the happy beat, not with boys who looked into the camera and sang about love as if their own hearts might break.

When the credits rolled, the words "London Weekend Television" confirmed what I suspected: everything valuable came from afar. I longed for the glamorous worlds of TV, the projects of *Good Times*, the high school of *Welcome Back, Kotter*, places where spoken words sounded like music and people with big personalities got lots of laughs.

Personality was on my mind that year, after I'd come across a quiz about it in a teen magazine. The multiple-choice answers were meant to determine whether a girl was a) outgoing, b) happy-go-lucky, c) shy and quiet, or d) serious yet romantic, with each answer corresponding to the sort of boy she should date. Fortune-telling held a lot of sway in our house, where my mother kept a dream interpretation book in the junk drawer, handy for looking up, say, "teeth falling out" and learning what would happen because of it. Astrology, Ouija boards, even the candle-lighting rituals of Catholicism offered a seductive mix of fate and agency, but the personality quiz was different. Three attempts revealed no pattern to my answers. None of the adjectives offered applied to me, and I couldn't think of another that did. The only logical conclusion was that I didn't have a personality. At eleven years old, I was a blank slate.

This realization sent me to the edge of despair and launched a period during which I holed up in my bedroom for long hours, listening to the radio and contemplating the nature of identity. Although it would take years for me to understand and claim the word "feminist," I believed women in the news, like Bella Abzug with her eccentric hats and the fiercely pretty Gloria Steinem, when they insisted that women and girls were equal to men and boys. I planned to go to college one day and have a career and demand equal pay for equal work, but what I wanted right then was to be "happy-go-lucky" or "serious yet romantic." I felt dull, bland, not worth the attention of anyone, including Greg Larson, the classmate I'd been in love with for three solid years.

Then came the late Saturday afternoon in December when the Bay City Rollers burst into the living room. The bouncy music, the weeping girls, the spectacle of it all both attracted and repelled me, and when the program ended, I went upstairs and lay down on my bed, shaking. I replayed the final song in my mind—"S-A, T-U-R, D-A-Y Night"—and felt the atmosphere of that stage, how the guys shook confetti out of their hair and the screaming girls launched themselves forward. Something I couldn't name twisted in my stomach, something scary and exciting, something that might offer a clue to my personality. Or maybe, I thought, the identity of "fan" could pass for personality until a more authentic one came along.

The *tink* of the light switch on my bedroom wall was as familiar a sound as my own voice, but what followed felt like an electric shock. After a month away, I saw the room as a stranger might: the narrow bed with its floral spread tucked over the pillow, the white dresser with gilded trim, the frosted-glass light fixture on the ceiling, all overshadowed by a riot of images. On each wall, from baseboard to ceiling, were faces, bodies, plaids, stripes, headshots, group shots, color centerfolds and black-and-white pinups, so many they nearly overlapped. I blinked and shook my head. This was the room of a crazy person.

"Come on!" Michael urged from his doorway, blond bangs covering his forehead and round face frowning above the stuffed turtle he was packing. His blue eyes widened as if trying to impress upon me the urgency of the situation.

I wanted to be kind, but I'd heard the single *whoop* of the squad car turning into our driveway. "The police are here," I said, and he dropped the turtle and headed for the stairs. I didn't follow. The neighbors—Irene and Tony, who gave out little bags of candy for Halloween, Terrie and Ed and their three kids, whose pool I had learned to swim in—would be out in their yards, watching. Kids across the street on the playground of the elementary school would be leaning against the fence and wondering what crime had been committed in our house. I wanted nothing to do with all that.

But the rhythmic flashing at the window motivated me. I reached for a color centerfold, the first poster I'd affixed to the wall back when the yellow paint was fresh. The band stood in a sunlit field, postures relaxed, looking like five of the sweetest, most promising guys in the world. They were nearly feminine in their beauty, arms draped over one another's shoulders, shirts open to the waist. Their clothes were white and red and pale denim, all trimmed in tartan, and everything about the field, the tall grass around their ankles, the sunlight falling through the trees and patting the tops of their hair, appealed to my sense of romance.

I peeled the poster from the wall, corner by corner, leaving dark smudges behind. Rubbing at them with my thumb and fingernail didn't help, and if the walls looked frightening with so many posters affixed, they would look both frightening and damaged when I was done. Each time my father glanced into this room, he'd see tiny bruises.

Just then his voice rose from the driveway. "What in the hell is going on here?"

Fear rippled along my skin, but I contained it, reasoning that the police would make sure no one got hurt. As daunting as all the posters now seemed, I could feel their power again and with it the relief of being a girl in love, someone possessed, obsessed in a way that felt like salvation.

There wasn't time to take everything, so I pried the life-sized head of my favorite guy, Woody, from the wall beside the bed, where I'd kissed it before falling asleep each night. Next came a glossy poster of his long body, naked except for a strategically placed plaid scarf, his boney hips as sexy as anything I'd seen. Then on to group shots. Some posters tore, corners clinging to the walls, while others piled up on the bed, their tape sticking to the pages above and below until everything was in danger of ruin.

The stairs creaked fast, and my father's wounded voice called out my name. He rushed to the doorway and stopped, out of breath, while I focused on the poster in my hand, on the bright colors and carefree expressions, on rolling a piece of tape off my finger. I didn't want to look at his wide face and solid build, but he stayed in the doorway until I turned toward him. His cheeks were sunken, etched with lines that weren't there a few weeks before, and his normally combed-back hair flopped onto his forehead as if he'd just woken up. I waited for him to scold me about the marks on the walls, but he just stared, blinking, and then he was gone again and my mother soon took his place. "Never mind the goddamned posters! Get your clothes."

I had planned to move faster on this mission. The girl I'd become in the past month didn't dilly-dally. She was helpful, responsible, keeping the kitchen clean and folding baskets of laundry each night. She kept an eye on the younger kids and sometimes made dinner, but she was also, secretly, a little weird. She didn't shower or change her underclothes every day, and this puzzled me. Each morning I woke determined to make a change, but when evening rolled around and the bathroom rotation began, I let the shower run while standing at the sink, brushing my teeth and splashing water on my face. When Maggie asked whether she might buy me some underpants, since there weren't many in the wash, I arranged my face into an expression of insult. "I have *lots*."

In fact, there was a week's worth in my duffel bag, and now I added three more pairs to a garbage bag filled with faces and records. I dragged the bag downstairs, through the gaping living room and empty dining room to the doorway of the kitchen, where the two older cousins were trying to push the stove out the back door as my father's strong, compact body held them at bay.

"The appliances are mine," my mother was telling the police officer outside. "I picked them out myself."

"How am I supposed to cook?" my father shouted from the back step, one shoulder pressed against the stove. "Where am I going to put my food?"

Timmy stood in the dining room, looking out the window at the back steps. When our eyes met, he flexed his neck as if to say, "Yikes."

The cop spoke calmly, like a judge. He understood that the stove and refrigerator belonged to my mother, but since her new apartment came with appliances and she didn't have anywhere to put these, wouldn't it be best to leave them for now? There was more discussion, more shouting, and more of the cop's measured tone, and eventually the two cousins jiggled the stove back to its place. Uncle Marty plugged the refrigerator in again.

"I can't believe this," my father kept saying. "You wanted me to come home from work tonight and find this? No stove or refrigerator? No way to live in this house?"

The aggrieved tone of my father's voice made my skin burn. He was right, of course. But at least he had a house, with a bathroom he didn't have to wait in line for. He had a yard and a washing machine and a dog I missed so much I couldn't go near him, tied out back, yelping his head off.

In the driveway, everyone milled around while my mother explained herself to the cop. "I left him because he hit me," she said. "Naturally I wasn't going to come when he was here. My lawyer advised me to do this."

"Your lawyer's a goddamned crook!" my father countered, because it was true, he had hit her. Two punches, late at night, and we took off. No one had expected the violence, not even my father, who sat on the couch until dawn waiting for the police to come arrest him. I didn't forgive him the punches, but I knew that my mother had taken up with Jan before we moved out, and that her denials had rattled my father to the core. He'd wanted to believe she wouldn't betray him, but the stories didn't add up. Why was she grocery shopping on Sundays all of a sudden and taking forever at it? The answer was that Maggie took her parents to church each Sunday, leaving Jan free to talk for an hour. While my mother huddled against the pay phone by the courtesy desk, I went aisle to aisle, ticking items off the list, pretending to shop for my Scottish boyfriend and imagining him looking at me the way Jan often looked at my mother.

Now, standing beside cousin Timmy in the dining room, it occurred to me that I was the only person who could see the whole situation for what it was because of something that must be a personality trait. I watched. I paid attention. I tucked information away and kept quiet about it, trying to make sense of the story in my head. Happy-go-lucky I was not. But observant? Good at keeping secrets? A spy, even?

It was dark by the time everything got sorted out. The living room chairs would go with us, the couch would stay. ("The man needs a place to sit," the police officer said with authority.) We could take the stereo and the dining room table and of course the kids' beds, but not the pots and pans, not the dishes, not the sheets for the double bed. ("You'll have to start over a little bit, too, ma'am.") Finally, with the truck full, my uncle and cousins squeezed into the cab and headed for our new apartment, where they would unload everything so that, the next afternoon, my mother and brother and I could begin setting up our home.

Meanwhile, the police officer stood in the driveway, scribbling notes on a pad. The dog continued to bark until my father put him in the house, where he lunged repeatedly against the dining room window. My father had to get back to work but the window on the back door was smashed so he couldn't lock the house. "God almighty," he said to the cop. "What was she thinking?"

While my father searched the garage for replacement glass, my mother told Michael and me to get in the car. And we would have, if Skipper hadn't continued lunging at the window, calling my brother to him. Just for one hug. Just to say goodbye. The moment the door opened, Skipper flew out, Michael's scrambling hands and legs no match for a dog's desire to join his pack. Skipper raced to my mother, dancing and barking and howling, the fur of his face wet with what looked like tears.

"Take the dog!" my father yelled over the noise. "Please, he's heartbroken! He shits all over the house and I have to keep him in the cellar. He doesn't understand!"

"I can't," my mother repeated, shaking her head and backing up as if she'd seen a ghost. The apartment complex didn't allow pets.

In the car, Michael scrunched beside bags in the back seat while I sat up front, pressing my forehead against the window. I watched Skipper wriggle against my father's grasp as we backed out of the driveway, watched as the dog broke free and began to run, determination pressing his ears flat against his head, and if this were a short story, I'd be tempted to let him catch up, to move him under the back wheel and enhance the tragedy. But Skipper didn't catch up, and he lived mostly in the cellar for the next couple of months until one weekend morning, when my father let him out and the dog, with no one around as his witness, ran straight into the path of a semi.

"Come back! Come back here right now!" my father yelled, chasing until we'd turned the corner.

We drove a few blocks in silence before my mother flicked open a cigarette lighter and gave a long exhale. I rolled the window down and stared at the passing street-lights, feeling the soft September night against my face. I was thinking that it's a terrible thing to break into some-one's home, legal or not, and that I could have prevent-ed the fiasco, could have convinced my mother it was a bad idea or threatened to tell my father. But I hadn't, and now I wasn't sure the possibility had even crossed my mind. All I remembered from the days leading up to this night was the excitement of being reunited with things that mattered. Things that gave me shape and depth, that reminded me of who I was and how deeply I loved, even when that love stood no chance of being returned. I'd wanted those things, and the force of that wanting had been bigger than anything around it.

All the way back to Jan and Maggie's house, I felt sad for my father, guilty about the evening's events, and excit-ed by a shift. Not long before, I'd been a girl who taped posters to the walls, a couple at first and then more and more as the months passed and the tensions grew, paper-ing herself into a kind of cocoon. Now I was someone else, someone whose personality involved keeping quiet, guarding secrets, becoming a repository of stories. But not forever. One day, I thought while planning the bubble bath I would soak in that night until my skin wrinkled, regardless of how many people banged on the door, one day I would tell on us all.

CRUSHED

There's a certain way with certain boys, how they walk, a little lop-sided, leaning into one another, how they grimace when their heads go back, laughing to the sky. While their friends wait in the hall, shoes screeching against the tile floor, these boys pack up slowly, smiling under their bangs. They say, "Have a good afternoon," and "Looking forward to reading Montaigne," with no sense of irony. Then they hoist their heavy backpacks over one shoulder, give a quick salute, and are gone.

At a certain age—twelve to fourteen, by fifteen it's over—these boys are dangerous. Outside during morning break, they sidle up, leaning into me the way they lean into each other, sensing how I love being in the middle of them. One in particular, Eli, takes my hand, adjusts my grip on the Frisbee, cheers when my toss reaches the far birch tree. He likes teaching the teacher.

At academic summer camp, where the overachievers go for fun, boys like Eli talk about literature, about the *pieces* they're working on, with an earnestness that throbs.

In the cafeteria at dinnertime, carrying trays piled with tater tots and chocolate pudding, they ask me to settle a bet. What's "Hills Like White Elephants" really about? Their eyes drop to the floor, feet shift back and forth. At night they come to me in dreams, and in the morning when I step into the classroom and their heads turn toward me, eyes sleepy, I am shy.

Most of the summer writing students want to be in Fiction Workshop. I teach its prerequisite, Personal Narratives, although I have no idea why this course should come first. We read Virginia Woolf, James Baldwin, Joan Didion and talk about developing a literary consciousness. About what it means to tell the truth. About memory and imagination, craft and technique. "But nothing worth writing about has ever happened to me," they sometimes whine. "The drama is in the way you think," I insist, and the dangerous boys nod their heads and grin.

We spend most of each day in a small, carpeted classroom: fifteen students, the teaching assistant, and me. We sit around an enormous seminar table where we discuss readings and do writing exercises. Every other day, three students distribute drafts for the whole class to critique, making the close quarters even more intimate. By the end of the first week, it feels like a month has passed.

In the evenings, during study time, I walk through the girls' dormitory first. The girls are twelve and thirteen and fourteen, too, but they seem older, less vulnerable. They have breasts and long legs, and some are so beautiful it's hard to look at them, hard to look away. A few apply makeup expertly and braid their hair into intricate patterns, but I don't compliment appearances. Instead I say, "I like the way you think. Push that idea further. Bring it up in class tomorrow so we can all learn from you."

This pleases the girls, but what they really want to talk about is the boys. They want to know if I'll tell so-and-so that so-and-so likes him, if I'll relay dares and threats about tomorrow morning's four-square match. "Nope," I reply, "no flirting by proxy," and the girls fall out laughing, squealing until the RA threatens to write them up.

The next dormitory is quieter. Up and down the halls, boys read and write and goof around silently. I make myself at home, sitting on a chair here, a bed there, and taking what they offer—Twizzlers, Cheetos, Coffee Nips. Eli's roommate received a care package today, and Eli gives of it freely. He just turned twelve, the youngest in the class, and he sits beside me on the narrow bed—elbows on his knees, hands clasped like some kind of professional—and asks about the college students I teach. What are they like, he wants to know, and what am I reading for pleasure? He shows me a wooden duck his grandfather carved and a bracelet he wove during afternoon activities. He opens his laptop to essay number one. "What do you think of this beginning?" he asks, and I'm not kidding, it's stunning.

The joke at nerd camp is you can tell new instructors by who doesn't show up to lunch the first day. That's what happened to me three years ago, after a friend, whose recommendation counted for more than it should have, got me the job. I had no idea how much these kids would know, how eagerly they'd devour lesson plans. I come from the kind of working-class, public-school background few of them share, so it didn't occur to me that by seventh grade they'd be versed in classical mythology or able to analyze a Van Gogh painting with lightning speed. On that first morning, my class ate through two days' worth of lessons. I spent lunch hour planning how to get to 3:00.

Now, halfway to a Ph.D. in English and grateful for this recurring summer job, I'm used to adolescents who know more than I do about calculus, molecular biology, the timelines of historic battles. And I'm also used to student writing that might be great for seventh grade but isn't, on its own, impressive. There's a slight, perverse pleasure in knowing that in one area, in *my* area, these kids don't necessarily excel. So Eli's opening paragraph takes me by surprise. I haven't had time to teach him yet.

During the first workshop, we discuss essays about a pet goldfish that died, a baby sibling who arrived like an angel from heaven, and a father who left his family for another man. About the goldfish and the sibling there is much to say. Great descriptions! So relatable! The same thing happened to my fish! I listen for a while, giving the shy students time to participate, and then ask, "What's this essay really about?" I look around the table, meeting their eyes. "Let's talk about ideas." The students gaze back. Some sit up a little straighter. Others twirl pens, snap gum, toy with the colorful bands on their braces. In a moment, ideas start to come, and before long even the author's conceding that the fish hadn't meant much to her, even at the time, but the ritualistic burial gave the backyard an aura of the sacred.

When we turn to the third essay, the one about the gay father, silence fills the room. I glance at the clock, prepared to wait a full minute before intervening. At the thirty-second mark, which is much longer at a workshop table than elsewhere, the teaching assistant Tina shifts in her chair and widens her eyes, begging me to intervene. I realize she's right, that the silence can't go on so long that the witty, awkward boy who wrote the essay starts to squirm.

But just as I'm about to speak, Eli clears his throat. "OK, well, I thought this was really brave and really moving. I mean, I got a little choked up at the end." He gives the author a quick smile, then flips through the pages, cocking his head to the side. "But . . ." Eli's face tightens with concentration. "I wanted to see more of your father. Especially before he told you he was gay. I wanted to spend time with him so I could feel your sadness when he left."

The author nods with the heady excitement of being taken seriously, and three new hands go up in the air. Watching these students—children, really, with their oversized tee shirts and budding acne—hold a mature conversation, speaking directly to the bespectacled boy who both loves and resents his father, moves me almost to tears.

In Eli's room that night I tell him what a great job he did in workshop. He nods and looks at the floor, lips pressed together against a smile. We're sitting side by side on his bed again, and I have the strong urge to drape my arm across his shoulder, pull him close, touch my lips to the short brown hair above his ear.

During the second week, on a lazy-hot afternoon that's perfect for a swim, our class fills the narrow computer lab. The lights are off and blinds open, creating the illusion of dim comfort, and the students click along the keyboards with type-A discipline. In the back row, Tina consoles a girl who started to cry while describing her brother's epilepsy. In the front row, Eli has fallen into a pattern of typing furiously and then deleting with a frustrated shake of his head.

"How's it going?" I ask, standing to the side so I can't see his screen.

Eli sighs. "Something's wrong here, but I don't know what." He scoots over and I perch beside him on the chair, our shoulders touching. He's right. Despite the stunning first paragraph, the essay lacks direction. I say, "It seems like you're circling around an idea you're also resisting."

"Exactly." Eli rubs a palm along his freckled cheek. His tee shirt smells faintly of fabric softener, a woven bracelet hangs on his thin wrist. "But what's the idea?"

I shove him a little with my shoulder. "It's your essay, you tell me."

Eli smiles, stares at the screen, wrinkles his brow.

After a moment, I point to a phrase. "OK, what about this girl right here? You say you didn't like her, but isn't this whole experience about trying to impress her?"

He leans forward and reads the sentence aloud. "Huh," he says.

"Could this be an essay about not understanding what you want? About . . . desire?" I pause, waiting for Eli to blush or fidget the way twelve-year-olds do, but his forefinger goes to his chin, taps lightly, and he starts to grin. Later I show him how to work the prose, using a sentence fragment here, parallel structure there, along with repetition so the music of the phrases carries meaning. "Excellent," Eli whispers, his mind wrapping around my words. He gets it, and he knows it came from me, and nothing, nothing else I do, is as seductive as this.

Nerd camp is filled with crushes. Kids pair up right and left, a Monday attraction developing and running its course—bad breakup, friendly reconciliation—by Wednesday. And of course there's a spate of student crushes on adults: girls flock around the handsome math teacher at lunch, boys wrestle in front of the kohl-eyed French TA. Attractions crop up in every class, across age and gender. By the end of the first week, campus is abuzz.

Which makes the middle of week two the perfect time to show the movie *Harold and Maude.* Every year this choice makes administrators nervous. They worry about the implied sex, the drugs, the suicide, but I argue that the film provokes kids into thinking hard, revising stereotypes, and asking good questions. I don't care whether students approve of a relationship between a young man and an elderly woman; I want to broaden the assumptions they make about the world.

On the appointed night, Tina and I hold study time in the classroom, pushing tables and chairs against the wall and allowing the students, who bring pillows and blankets, to sprawl on the floor. We dole out popcorn and candy, then sit back and watch everyone squirm. "What?" they gasp in unison when the romance becomes clear. Harold is the age of their older brothers! Maude is like their great-grandmothers! It's scandalous, nauseating, incomprehensible, or would be if Maude weren't so vibrant and inspiring. By the end of the film, we're all a little bit in love with her.

When Tina turns the lights on again, the students blink and shake their heads, then chatter as they pick up wrappers and gather their bedding. One girl jokes that she is no way telling her parents about this one, while a boy insists that even if the gender roles *were* reversed, it would still be disgusting. Other students counter, insisting that Harold was probably eighteen, what's the harm? Love is love, they sing, because it's summer and social hour starts in fifteen minutes on the quad. All's well, I think, humming to the Cat Stevens soundtrack. Then Eli appears at my

elbow, positioning himself so only I can hear and leaning in as if to tell me a secret. "That was a-MAY-zing," he
says, and the look on his face is one I've seen before. It's
the look of someone standing in a dark doorway, or sitting
in a parked car, someone about to slip a hand around my
waist and guide me toward him. For a moment it's hard
to remember where I am, and who this boy is in front of
me, with his confidence, his longing. Eli steps back, still
looking at me, still smiling, and the intense flush of his
cheeks makes my own face burn.

Walking back to the instructors' dorm, I think about
Eli's perspective. It's his summer vacation, after all. He's
been looking forward to camp for months, and there's not
a girl out of the hundred here who interests him. The older
ones, maybe, the sixteen-year-olds, but he's so small, so
wiry they don't take him seriously. It's early August, the
days already shortening, and the evening breeze carries
the scent of pine, a premonition of autumn woodsmoke
rolling down from the mountains. The week after next Eli
will be back home again, bored.

And it's my summer vacation, too. Inhaling that soft,
fragrant air, marveling at the silhouetted peaks, the sher-
bet sky, I feel loneliness settle in my hips. I have friends
here, people who teach writing, politics, archaeology,
chemistry, and most evenings we get together to eat and
drink and laugh about these brainiac kids. Some of us
come back year after year. We egg each other on, develop
history, have encounters and flings and full-blown affairs,
managing the restless energy.

Still, the energy of these certain boys, who think hard
and run fast and seem both younger and more mature
than they are, affects me. I'm old enough to be Eli's parent, the person who tells him he can't go to the mall and
has to finish his homework before watching TV. But I'm

not his parent. I'm a teacher who spends six hours a day with his class, and not once have I had to reprimand him or tell him to pay attention or remind him to do an assignment. In a group of astonishing kids, he's the standout. Twelve years old, small for his age, smart and sweet and more together than some men I know. Sometimes, when I watch him joking with his friends on the quad, the way they lean into each other, shove each other, laugh and then get serious for a moment, my throat tightens with some emotion I can't understand. Or maybe it's a combination of emotions: mournful love, buoyant sorrow, the outline of desire perched between an unknown future and the enigmatic web of the past.

At the end of the second week, Tina and I linger after class. Tina is the opposite of me in every way: tall, blonde, graceful, and charmingly on task. She's the disciplinarian in our room, with a low tolerance for the chaos that often erupts. Today she organizes files of lesson plans on the side table while I select a few essays for her to grade. We're chatting about the day, recounting funny moments and marveling at how lively workshop discussions have become. The conversation turns to Eli, how insightful he is, how attuned to his classmates. "He's the opposite of Tom Hanks in *Big*," Tina says, "a thirty-year-old man in a little boy's body."

We chuckle and fall silent. Then Tina lowers her voice and confesses: "Just between us, and I'm talking serious confidentiality here, OK? I'm crushing hard on Eli." Tina shakes her head, embarrassed, and wonders whether she's reverting to adolescence in this atmosphere. I let a moment pass, deciding how to respond, and then give in. "It's not just you."

We close the door and laugh ourselves breathless. He's twelve! And looks ten! We joke that he'll be legal in six years—how old will we each be then? Tina will be twenty-five, I'll be thirty-six. She calls dibs.

I point out that if we overheard two male teachers talking this way, the guys next door, for example, who have the fifteen-year-olds, we'd raise the roof. "No kidding," Tina says with a shudder. "That would not be cool at all."

That night we hold study time in the computer lab, after which everyone languidly crosses the quad. Tina and I are bringing up the rear, planning tomorrow morning, when Eli jogs back through the dusk. He left his Frisbee in the classroom earlier and really wants it for the morning, can we please, please let him get it? Of course, we say. The three of us head back to the building and when we come outside again, the other kids have hurried into the dorms to get ready for social hour and the quad is empty. Soon this green space will be filled, from ivy-covered wall to ivy-covered wall, with desperately eager teens.

As we walk, Eli talks about a short story we discussed this afternoon. It makes perfect sense to him that Miss Emily slept beside her dead suitor all those years, because she couldn't bear the loss, the *permanence* of it, you know? That's what's so hard. His voice is earnest, pained, a knife grazing my skin.

Tina glances over, and I shake my head, looking upward as if searching for strength. She laughs and breaks into a jog. "Come on, Eli, school's out for the day. Throw me that Frisbee!"

He does, and Tina catches it high above her head, then launches it to me. I pause before throwing while Eli and Tina both run backward waving their arms. I aim between them and they sprint, Eli catching the Frisbee half a second before Tina catches him, her long arms wrapping around his waist and lifting him into the air. He howls with laughter as she spins once, twice, then slows down, faces me, and sets him on the ground, her mouth pantomiming a scream and palms rising in a gesture that says, "I didn't do anything." For many years this tableau will come back to me: Eli holding the Frisbee and laughing, enjoying our attention, while Tina mocks her own impulse, fingers splayed to assert an innocence that doesn't quite exist.

Innocence doesn't exist. Complexity is everywhere. On paper, Personal Narratives is about structuring essays, using active verbs, developing main ideas, but in practice, the only idea I care about is that life is complicated. People are complicated. Emotions are beyond complicated, worming and turning and transforming, probing and circling back again. At the end of three weeks, I want these bright, privileged students to know what they only sensed before: that it's possible to feel joy and sorrow at once, to be both good and bad, to want and not want at the same time. That the opposite of love is not hate, the opposite of desire is not revulsion. The opposite of every emotion worth having is indifference.

And indifference there is, in week three. All over nerd camp, broken hearts have healed and hardened. "I don't care," the students say, walking into the classroom. "He's lame anyway." "Whatever." When Tina and I divide the class into small groups for certain lessons, we strategize about who's still getting along.

A few students sidestep the drama, among them Eli. Tina and I can't understand this. How can no one be interested in charming Eli? At breakfast we scan the cafeteria for someone deserving of his affection, and when we head to the classroom I hold my breath for a moment. I keep waiting for Eli to become infatuated with a girl or to discover the attraction of Tina, toward whom several of the boys and most of the girls in our class gravitate at every break. But Eli behaves in week three as he did on day one, smiling with delight when I call the class to order, as if being here, and having me for a teacher, is a prize he didn't expect to win.

On the penultimate night of camp, when I visit the boys' dorm during study time, Eli opens his dresser drawer and pulls out a gift. It's a bracelet woven from purple, red, and green yarns, the pattern more intricate than most. He ties it around my wrist, smiling, then looks me in the eye and with breathtaking gravity says, "The others were practice for this one."

I pull on my professional face, the one that allows me to speak when emotion balloons inside my ribs, and say, "It's gorgeous. Thank you." Then I turn to Eli's roommate, the boy with the care packages, the athlete over whom some of the girls are bickering. "OK, slacker, what have *you* got for me?" I ask, and while both boys fall on their beds laughing, I flee.

After my rounds I go looking for Tina, who is playing pool at a bar in town. When I walk in she's holding a beer and a cigarette and smiling sheepishly because she's underage, but I don't care about that. I raise my wrist and shake it so the bracelet slips along my arm.

"Oh my God!" Tina wails. "I never stood a chance!" We don't explain what's so funny, not to the teaching assistants she's with, not to the math teacher who might come back to my room tonight. Tina and I are role-playing, and also not, and her reaction intensifies the pleasure I feel at being chosen.

And it really is a pleasure. I want Eli to like me best, as ridiculous as that sounds. Because I like everything about him. The way he thinks, the way he smiles, the kindness in his voice when he offers workshop criticism that could come from a graduate student. I like watching the awkward way he walks, taking long steps to keep up with the bigger boys, and the speed of his run, which is somehow faster than everyone else's. I especially like the way he looks at me at the end of each afternoon, when he hoists that huge backpack over his shoulder and pauses to say, "Thank you for a great day." Every afternoon he says this, and yes it's polite, but he means it, too. He is a grateful boy, and I have the sense that, with the merest luck, he will grow into a grateful man. But that future man is not part of my crush. It's little Eli, here and now, whom I adore.

A crush is about desire, longing, wanting something, but what on earth do I want from a twelve-year-old? Or from any of the dangerous boys I teach each summer? During study hour, as I sit beside Eli on his bed, talking about the arc of a narrative, parallel scenes spin out in my imagination. With his roommate turned away, Eli takes my hand and squeezes it. Or brushes the hair off my face. Or, when I'm feeling particularly daring, our heads bend together over a page, faces turn, and lips lightly brush.

That's where the fantasy stops. Backtracks. Finds solid ground once again. I don't want to kiss Eli, not the way adults kiss each other. I don't even want to kiss him the way kids kiss each other, the way as a kindergartner I wanted to peck Danny Rodriguez's round cheek. Maybe all I want with Eli is what already exists: the light yet palpable connection that hums between us whenever we're in the same room. I want that hum, that fleeting, young-boy energy to aim itself, for this brief spell, toward me. Even more, I want to be carried along on its optimism through the rest of this summer and the rest of graduate school and into the unimaginable life that waits beyond. It's an impossible desire, I know. But the knowing does not make it go away.

Personal Narratives ends just before lunch on Friday. That's when parents appear, packing dorm rooms and loading minivans and lining up in the hallways for conferences. Tina plays emcee outside our classroom while I admit one set of parents at a time, close the door, and tell versions of the same story: She's a great kid, an excellent writer. He's a great kid, a terrific writer, but easily distracted. She's a great kid, a hard worker, and I'm sure her writing will mature over time. The parents are eager and nervous and proud. They have no idea what I know about them.

Eli's parents come near the end. They're so young, my goodness, we really are peers, and I can tell immediately—by their sneakers and tee shirts, their comfortable stances—that they're not going to ask whether this program will help him get into Harvard. They're solid, sensible people who just wanted him to do something he loves this summer. The father is tall and wiry, the mother petite. Eli is the perfect mix of their features.

I tell them he's extraordinary and they nod politely, clearly used to hearing how great their son is. They don't get it. They have no idea. So I take an extra minute and explain that every last kid on this campus is exceptional, OK? That what I'm saying is not the same as what his middle school teachers have said. I don't mean he's a genius. What I mean is that he has something, some mix of sensibility and insight and desire, that sets him apart. Their eyes widen, their faces color. I jot down the name of an online college writing course that can challenge him during the year, and we shake hands. As they turn to leave, Eli's mother stops and says, "He *adores* you," with a tone that seems—am I imagining it?—concerned. So I pull on my professional face and nod. "This was a good class."

When I open the door to let them out, Eli squeezes in. "You were eavesdropping," I admonish, ruffling his hair the way adults do to children and regretting it immediately because this is not how things have been between us. There's a pleading expression on his face, and he speaks quickly at first, then slower, with determination. "I know other people are waiting and I'm sorry, I don't want to take up your time, but this class has meant the world to me. It really has. And I just want to say, *thank you.*"

Eli extends his hand toward me, mother and father beaming, and I don't want this to happen but it does. My eyes begin to fill. Because tomorrow, as I start the two-day drive back to my real life, which does not include unlimited meals and linen service and youthful possibility stretching in every direction, I will miss him. Him, specifically, the most impressive by far of all the dangerous boys.

I blink, shake Eli's hand, meet his eye for a quick second and step toward the door. "I've enjoyed working with you," I say, and then his mom guides his shoulders, dad right behind, and there isn't time to catch my breath before the next father fills the doorway.

Heartache is a cliché that is also true, in many situations. My chest feels so tender that I press my left hand against it while extending the right to shake the next man's hand, and suddenly here he is again. Eli! He worms around the man in the doorway, ducks under the outstretched arms, and before I know what's happening, he's crushed against me. His cheek presses to my chest, hair brushes my chin, arms grasp my waist and hold on.

The next father watches. Eli's parents return. And Eli and I embrace in a way that should stop and doesn't. And still doesn't. It occurs to me that Eli is taking control of this story, changing the outcome, moving toward some kind of closure and taking me with him. I know that his feelings this summer aren't entirely about me: I'm the messenger, the teacher who embodies what he loves about this place where, for the first time in his life, he doesn't have to hide how smart he is, how much he thinks, how deeply he values literature and art and the capabilities of his own mind. I'm starring in this episode of his coming of age story, just as he's standing in for all the smart, sweet, not-yet-overbearing boys I love to teach, in my own story of figuring out who to position at the center of my life.

Finally, I let go and take a step back. Eli's eyes are moist, but he squares his shoulders and gives a satisfied, soldierly nod. "I didn't want to leave here without doing that," he says. And how do I feel? Grateful. For his maturity and sweetness. For his courage. And for this moment of genuine, inexplicable connection between a thirty-year-old teacher and a twelve-year-old boy, with his parents looking on.

ABOUT WAYNE

Romance stories are everywhere. They weave through our lives, catching us in their delicate strands, in their sometimes simple and sometimes intricate patterns. Whether we like it or not. Whether we even know it at the time.

On the mild winter day when my mother, brother, and I moved into a house with Jan and her three kids, our story was tender and new. The mothers were in love. The kids were cooperative. The three-bedroom cape in the country, eight miles from where I'd been raised, would be the antidote to a period of crisis. As we unloaded the borrowed van, everyone was polite, considerate, eager to be a family. Jan's oldest son Brian let my brother Michael choose which side of their attic bedroom to sleep on, and I encouraged her daughter to put her bed beside the window of our alcove at the top of the stairs. Each of the mothers took me aside that day to praise my kindness.

This was before the story began to shift, before my father got serious about the word "unfit," before Brian and Michael started to fight and I started to hang out with the girls at school who smoked weed in the bathroom. It was way before I realized that Wayne sometimes sat on our front steps in the dark, listening for bits of my conversation from inside, before he started leaving love notes in scratchy boy's handwriting pinned outside the door.

Wayne lived a quarter mile down the street, on the other side of some woods, and on that first day he rode his bike back and forth as we unloaded the van. He wore a hooded sweatshirt in place of a coat and pedaled quickly, then slowly, then quickly again, ignoring us on one pass and staring on the next. He reminded me of the kids in my old neighborhood, boys who called each other "faggot" and "jerk-off" and labeled each girl "fat ass." From the first moment I saw Wayne I thought, *stay away.*

But as I learned over the next months, Wayne wasn't as bad as those other boys. He'd steal from his parents' liquor cabinet and drop the f-word in front of the principal, then laugh about it on the late bus home after detention, but he never hit anybody or called us names. He didn't have the kind of mean streak I was used to.

What he did have was a romantic streak. Each day after school he and Michael and Brian would spend a couple hours messing around in the front yard, and if I joined them Wayne would turn goofy. He'd smile too much, skid his bike along the icy street until he landed on his side, go red in the face when I talked to him. So I mostly stayed away, either doing homework inside or skating on the pond behind the farmhouse across the street. Once winter turned the corner toward spring, I spent part of each afternoon hanging out with the farmer's cow, who lived in a tiny barn beside our house. I'd scratch her forehead and feed her weeds that had begun to sprout along the fence, taking solace in the only creature lonelier than I was.

By then we'd assumed the shape of a working-class Brady Bunch, minus the housekeeper and with a lot more attitude. My mother and Jan were the exhausted parents, Brian and I were the know-it-alls, and the younger kids were each certain they deserved more—more attention, more affection, more play time, more dessert—than they were getting. Even Jan's five-year-old, the only one of us to get a bedroom to himself, talked back every chance he got. In some ways I was the worst of the bunch, acting out not with sass but with eye rolls and withering stares, but at least I did things around the house. The other kids, I thought, were dead weight.

That's the story I was telling myself when April rolled around, a version of Cinderella in which I starred, toiling away while the other kids goofed off and the mothers failed to notice. But then spring break arrived, and for one magical day, everything changed.

At 10 a.m., the sun was bright and the house silent. I crept downstairs, surprised to have slept so late, and said hello to Jan's mother, whom everyone called Ma. I liked Ma, a no-nonsense woman with a wrinkled face that didn't smile unless something tickled her, but I wasn't crazy about spending each day of spring break with her. While my mother and Jan thought we kids would be fine on our own, Ma had argued that the older ones needed a vacation, too, they didn't need to spend their week babysitting. I had to agree with that, but the oversight made me nervous. What if I couldn't hold my sharp tongue? What if my brother and Brian started fighting and Ma couldn't break it up? What if she was like a substitute teacher, someone whose very presence antagonized us?

The past few weeks had been typical of April in the Hudson Valley, wet and chilly with occasional snow flurries, but overnight the weather changed. Now a warm breeze floated through open doors and windows, and the smell of cinnamon swirled through the kitchen.

Ma had made French toast for the other kids, and when I said hello, she got up from the armchair where she'd been reading the newspaper and started cooking, refusing my offer of help. I stood looking out the back door, toward a greening lawn and woods where tiny buds lined branches. I wanted to make conversation but didn't know what to say, until Ma finally asked if I'd ever had the chicken pox.

The chicken pox? A swirl of nostalgia enveloped me, and the breeze, the cinnamon, the question she'd asked in such a matter-of-fact way made me dizzy enough to take hold of the door jamb. Three years before, during an April like this one, I'd come down with the chicken pox and had a wonderful time. The first day was feverish and itchy, but after that, calamine lotion kept the spots in check while I missed ten glorious days of school. During that time the weather softened, our new color television set arrived, and I held forth in the living room recliner, watching game shows and soap operas and eating whatever was brought to me. I remembered the soft breeze that blew through the house and the sounds of my mother cooking a mid-day meal in the kitchen while my father got ready for work. From upstairs came the splashes of shaving, his deep voice humming old army songs and Patsy Cline. Later, after we ate—my parents in the kitchen and me in the recliner with a plate on my lap— my father brought me a peeled navel orange and held his hand against my forehead to make sure the fever hadn't returned. I remembered his concern, his tenderness, and what it felt like to accept without question the place my brother and I occupied at the center of our parents' lives.

I told Ma that Michael and I had both had the chicken pox, and she asked me to go look at Jan's youngest son and tell her what I thought.

The five-year-old was asleep in his bed, long eyelashes folded against his ruddy skin and angry spots dotting his face and arms. For months I'd considered this kid the biggest pest in the world, but watching him now, face relaxed and breath quiet, I felt sorry, the kind of sorry that starts small and, if you dwell on it, becomes an umbrella, a canopy, an overarching compassion for everyone and everything. Chicken pox during spring break meant the poor kid wouldn't get a sick day off of school.

Back in the kitchen, I asked Ma where the others were, and she said out riding bikes with Wayne. I imagined them tearing down the road or along trails in the woods, stopping to catch salamanders by the creek, and thought about joining them. But lately Wayne had been telling anyone who'd listen how much he liked me, and I didn't want to encourage him.

When I sat down to eat, Ma pushed a folded-up piece of notebook paper toward me. "I found this clothespinned to the bush outside the front door," she said. "It's addressed to you."

I grimaced in an exaggerated way. The note thing had been going on for about three weeks, mostly on weekends when Wayne wouldn't have to face me at the bus stop the next morning. I'd told Brian, which effectively meant I'd told Wayne, that I wasn't interested, but Wayne wasn't giving up. I flattened the page against the table and read aloud that I was beautiful, that Wayne loved me, and that he really wanted to hang out with just me once in a while. "Give me a break," I said, rolling my eyes.

Ma smiled and started filling the sink, while I silently read the note again. In the upper right corner of the page was a number ten, circled. I showed it to Ma, who said it must be the tenth note I'd gotten. I said no, it was maybe the fifth, and then Ma wondered if he'd meant to put ten notes on the bush all at once. "*Ten* notes?" I said. "Believe me, Wayne Johnson does not have that kind of energy." Ma thought that was very funny, and as we laughed together, the sweet breeze floating along our arms and necks, spring seemed to have arrived in spades.

"We tell ourselves stories in order to live," Joan Didion famously wrote. And we revise those stories, too, in a life-long process of trying to understand. The earliest story I remember telling myself involved an imaginary friend, Mrs. Cookus, who appeared alongside the arrival of my brother before I was three and stayed for a couple of years. Mrs. Cookus was an elderly woman, spry and cheerful and indulgent, and she never tired of playing or of telling me how special I was. In the narrative of my life at the time, Mrs. Cookus appeared because I deserved her.

By the time Ma appeared on the first day of spring break, I'd long outgrown jealousy over a younger sibling, but the sense of being pushed out of the center of my mother's life was strong. While I enjoyed that my mother was in love and felt loved and had a partner, anger sometimes overwhelmed my approval and made me dwell on everything that was wrong in our lives. My mother and I never talked anymore without an audience. The well water in this house smelled like sulphur. My father was suing for custody.

Into all of that came Ma, a real-life version of Mrs. Cookus. She did loads of laundry, made a pile of tuna sandwiches for lunch, scrubbed the bathroom, mopped the kitchen floor. When I offered to help, she said, "No, honey, it's too nice a day. Go outside and enjoy yourself." Instead, I sat on the couch with a notebook, pretending to work on a school project and answering Ma's questions. How was school going? (Okay). Why didn't I visit my best friend anymore? (Because she had a new best friend who lived closer to her, in my old neighborhood). Was I nervous about the custody hearing in two weeks? (Maybe a little.) She also asked whether I thought it would be all right for us to move the TV into the five-year-old's room so he could watch cartoons from the comfort of his bed. I told her that was a great idea, even though Jan's rule was that if you're sick, you rest; you don't watch TV. Despite my parents' differences, one thing they'd always agreed on was that sick kids belong in front of the TV, eating whatever they crave.

Finally, Ma asked about Wayne. She was dusting the coffee table by then, and I had moved to the green recliner, notebook open in my lap. Brian and Michael asked me the same questions every night—what about Wayne? what's wrong with Wayne?—and every night I told them to shut their big mouths. But Ma's questions were different. She wasn't trying to convince me to like Wayne; she was trying to figure out what kind of boy interested a girl like me.

I couldn't answer that question. I knew it wasn't Wayne, and it wasn't Jeff Hill, either, who earlier that year had passed me a note during English class, its message written in thick letters made by an unsharpened pencil: "Want to go out with me?" I pretended to think about it for a minute, then wrote, "No thanks," and handed it back. After class, I told Jeff's best friend that Jeff was cute but I liked someone else, so they wouldn't be mad at me, but really it was the way those pencil marks looked, so large and eager, that turned me off. Although Wayne used a pen for his notes, the handwriting reminded me of Jeff's, both of them liking me without knowing why, wanting something even they didn't understand.

Ma asked again about Wayne, and because she seemed genuinely interested, I decided to tell her what I hadn't told the boys. "He's gross. He spits all the time and doesn't wear a coat."

Ma laughed. "Spitting I can see. But maybe Wayne doesn't have a coat."

"He does," I insisted. "He carried it with him on the really cold days, but he only put it on once."

Ma rubbed the dust cloth over one of my mother's knick-knacks, a pair of ceramic hands clasped in prayer, and set it back on the stereo cabinet. "What do you care if he doesn't wear a coat? Maybe he doesn't get cold."

I inhaled deeply and shook my head for the exhale. "He was always cold in the winter. He'd be shivering at the bus stop, with his hands shoved way down in his pockets, except when he was smoking, and then he tucked the hand with the cigarette under the other arm so the cigarette stuck out in back." I stood up and assumed Wayne's hunched position, not bothering to explain that he wore flannel shirts with quilted flannel shirts over them, plaid on plaid, and a bandana around his neck, but he was still cold, still sniffling and stomping his work boots in the snow, his face and fingers bright red. "I'm not going out with anybody who doesn't know enough to keep himself warm," I said, curling a foot under me as I sat down again.

Ma turned to face me, one hand on her hip and the other holding the cloth, her eyes narrowed to slits. I regretted telling her Wayne smoked and wanted to explain that "going out" didn't mean we'd actually go anywhere, but then her stern face cracked into a smile and she said, "Does your mother have any idea how smart you really are?"

"Nope," I said, and we laughed long and hard.

The one bit of help Ma accepted that day involved waiting on the sick child. I brought him lunch in bed and offered to play a board game, which seemed to make him both happy and suspicious. Throughout the afternoon I moved between the kitchen at one end of the house and his bedroom at the other, carrying snacks and drinks. The other kids were in the front yard with Wayne for a lot of that time, and I knew he could see me as I walked through the living room. From certain angles in the yard, the front door aligned with a picture window on the back wall, and the house became transparent. At night, when my mother clothes-pinned the curtains together before curling onto the couch with Jan, who held her hand, stroked her hair, kissed her tenderly during commercials, the living room seemed like a hiding place. But during the afternoon, with Wayne pining away for me in the front yard, it felt like a stage.

I was on that stage, carrying a glass of 7-Up, when my mother and Jan got home from work. Wayne, Brian, and Michael were standing by the edge of the road, their heads bent over Wayne's hands, and the way Jan veered around them and sped into the driveway made me pause and watch. The car hardly came to a rest before the passenger's door flew open and my mother stomped toward the boys. I looked harder to see what Wayne was holding, because it seemed that whatever it was had angered my mother. It did not seem logical, or even possible, that I was involved.

My mother shouted but I couldn't make out her words, and Wayne stepped backward toward the road, my mother's hands waving and pointing in the direction of his house. Jan approached and took her arm. Then Brian ran toward our house, up the steps and through the door calling my name, but he didn't have time to explain before my mother came in the door behind him and Jan behind her, while Ma and I stood side by side, staring.

My mother didn't lose her temper often. She ignored a lot of things, did a slow burn about others, and then once in a while exploded. This was one of those times. Throwing her purse onto the table, she glared at me, then shouted that she wasn't going to put up with this, goddamn it. Ma and I looked at each other, my confusion mirrored in her arched eyebrows. "Rita," Ma said gently, "she doesn't know what you're talking about."

My mother didn't listen. She paced back and forth, living room to kitchen to hallway, and Jan followed her with a worried face, pausing only to ask what had happened to the TV.

My mother looked like she might cry, eyebrows furrowed and chin wrinkling, but she continued to shout about working hard and doing her best and not being able to watch me every minute. My stomach tightened the way it used to when I woke in the middle of the night to my father's booming voice, my mother's high-pitched comebacks, the sound of ashtrays rattling on the kitchen table. I felt dizzy, confused by what this story, which

I'd thought I understood, was turning into. I set the glass of 7-Up down on the counter as the words "Stop it!" screeched from my mouth, and in the startled silence that followed, I flew upstairs.

Ma was right. Wayne had written ten notes. And the night before the first day of spring break, he pinned all ten to the juniper bush outside our front door to show how much he cared for me. When my mother and Jan left for work in the morning they saw the notes, and my mother plucked one off the bush and got a glimpse into the way twelve- and thirteen-year-olds sometimes talked even then, in that time before social media and online access to pornography, when enterprising kids found ways of fueling their imaginations and seducing one another. Or trying to.

Horrified, my mother had taken all the notes, accidentally missing number ten, and spent the whole day thinking about how to deal with the problem. She and Jan devised some course of action, but when they got home and saw Wayne in the yard, my mother lost her mind. She told him to get off our property, leave her daughter alone, never speak to me again, never walk on the road in front of our house again, or she would kill him. "She threatened to *kill* Wayne, right out on the street!" Brian marveled, after following me up the stairs and explaining everything, the dirty notes and the threats my mother had made. I almost laughed at how ridiculous it all was, but something in Brian's expression, his wide-eyed smile, his obvious enjoyment of the drama, stopped me. "Go away," I hissed, and he said, "Geez, lighten up," and I hissed again, louder this time, "Get out of here, dirt bag."

I was angrier than I'd thought possible, because Ma had made French toast for breakfast and it was the warmest day since October and spring break had started out better than I could have imagined and then, all of a sudden, the story changed the way everything lately kept changing without warning.

Soon the stairs creaked and my mother appeared. She sat down on the end of the bed, a pile of folded papers in her hand. I alternated between glaring at her and glaring at my posters on the slanted ceiling until, finally, she said in a pleading voice, "Honey, you can't believe how filthy those letters were. I had no idea Wayne was like that."

I felt the sympathy umbrella begin to open again and struggled to snap it shut. I wanted to say, "They're *all* like that, Mother, all the boys I know," even though I had never called her "Mother" before. I wanted to use the language of after-school specials in which heart-wrenching episodes turned out okay. Instead, I said, "Give me the notes. They were addressed to me." She said no, she didn't want me reading that stuff, and I said, "They're mine, and this is none of your business." She said, "*You* are my business," and I replied, with perfect TV annunciation, "No, I am not."

After a long silence, my mother's eyes began to glisten, and she handed over one note, watching as I skimmed the page to see what could possibly be so bad. In letter number six Wayne had copied a table, which he footnoted as coming from a men's magazine, outlining the number of calories burned during various sexual acts. Blow jobs were on the list, along with sex while standing, and intercourse had been broken into three levels: slow, medium, and vigorous, but I didn't pay attention to the exact calorie counts because I was too busy wondering if Wayne Johnson thought I was fat.

Then I saw what had shocked my mother. Below the table lay a series of questions about my sexual preferences. Did I like giving blow jobs? What about having sex while standing? Wayne's assumption that I *had* sexual preferences was strangely flattering, given that I'd never even kissed a boy, but I could see that the possibility had undone my mother.

I kept my face very still as I read, determined not to show surprise or disgust or pleasure. I wanted my mother to worry, to take an interest in my life the way she used to, rather than paying attention only when some nonsense from a gross boy came along.

When I'd finished reading and looked at my mother, the tears in her eyes sat balanced above the bottom lashes, not escaping, and for a moment she seemed confused, like she couldn't remember how we got here or how to go back. And then I couldn't remember either, and some of my anger began to seep away. I looked down at the page, trying to think of a response that would return this day to normal. When I glanced up again, my mother's face had changed. In place of anger there was relief, the hint of a smile, as if she'd seen the truth in the way I read the note, as if I couldn't possibly be the kind of girl Wayne thought I was. Her brow had relaxed, her confidence returned. I imagined her thinking I didn't know what a blow job was because she'd never defined it for me.

I said, "These letters were my problem, and I would have handled it."

"Well, now you don't have to." There was a finality to her voice, as if she'd done me a favor.

That was it. I crumpled note number six and flung it just past her hand, onto the floor. "Come back here!" my mother called, but I was already down the stairs and rushing through the kitchen. My fury almost softened when Ma appeared, but Jan stepped behind her as if poised to intervene, and then the back door was slamming hard and I was running, down the steps, across the yard, onto a trail through the woods.

Romantic storylines often follow curious paths, dark and overgrown one moment and in the next, transformed by space and light. Taboos give way to passion, resistance to embrace. We'd read *Romeo and Juliet* in English class that year, and as I sat on a log, tossing twigs into the stream, I considered the allure of forbidden love, the us-versus-the-world excitement felt by Shakespeare's young couple and also, I imagined, by my mother and Jan. Their inter-actions were friendly in public or when anyone, including Ma, visited our home. But once the outsiders were gone and it was just us, two moms and five kids, they transformed into an amorous couple, their desire a secret we all silently agreed to keep. I longed for the intensely romantic, determined quality of the love they shared.

That could easily have been the storyline for Wayne and me. If the boy my mother had run off our property were even a little bit appealing, I would have seen him as my hero. Didn't she know that? Hadn't she learned from TV movies that the worst way to deal with an adolescent girl was by pushing her into the arms of a rebel boy?

The sun dipped below the hillside, casting an orange glow across the stream. I thought about how volatile my mother had become lately. One night a month before, she'd taken a belt to Michael's backside, something Jan encouraged because of his constant mouthing off. My mother had spanked us when we were younger, but being hit with a belt hadn't been remotely possible in our old life, and that night, as I lay on my bed listening to my ten-year-old brother beg for mercy, I felt sick with complici-ty. I knew I should go downstairs and do something to make her stop, but I also knew that none of the old rules applied now, that it was possible, in trying to make things better, to make them worse instead. Afterward, Michael's behavior improved for a couple of weeks before he hardened to the notion of punishment. "What are you going to do, beat me?" he'd say when my mother's temper flared, and I couldn't help admiring his obstinance.

Sitting at the edge of the stream, I imagined saying outright what I'd been thinking these last few weeks: "You're not a good mother anymore." That would sting her, all right. That would show her the depth of my unhappiness. But just below the surface of that anger was an indulgent self-pity that bubbled up the longer I sat alone. Three years before, on a day like today, I'd had the chicken pox and felt happy, cared for. Now I felt the opposite. Crying might have been cathartic, but I wasn't even close to tears. As the sun faded and the water trickled past and the air cooled, my self-pity grew. I poked at the ground with a twig and lay my cheek against my knee in the pose of someone wronged, imagining that if Ma could see me, Ma who asked questions and listened to the answers and who thought I was smart and knew I was innocent, she would feel heartbroken.

I thought about the custody hearing in two weeks, about how determined my father was to have us live with him. I thought about the echo in his half-empty house, about my old bedroom, its carpet sun-faded except where the bed and dresser used to be. On our visits every few weekends, my father asked questions. *Do you like Jan? Does she ever yell at you? How many bedrooms in that house? Who shares?* What he really wanted to know was whether my mother and Jan slept together, and if he'd asked me straight out I would have wrinkled my eyebrows like he was crazy and hoped he didn't push it. Instead he hinted, and I stewed because no one ever asked me what I wanted, they just talked to the lawyers and to each other, sniping about who was at fault.

I didn't know then that a few nights before the custody hearing, my mother would take me aside and explain that the judge wanted to talk to me and that I would have to lie to him about her relationship with Jan. "Otherwise your father will win," she'd say, watching my face intently for agreement. When I nodded slowly, thinking that maybe we should just tell the truth—because why couldn't two women raise kids together? why shouldn't we all be a family?—my mother saw the doubt on my face and knew what it meant. The next day she went to my father, offered to reconcile, made plans to move us back to our old house, where she'd be unhappier than ever and where I would long for the woods, the pond across the street, the cow, and even the chaos of a house with five kids and two parents in love.

Before all that happened, I sat for a long time beside the creek, wishing my mother would come looking for me. I wanted to be her pride and joy, her priority, her friend. She'd always thought of me as a good kid, and I would be, I decided. If she'd just come into the woods to find me, I'd be nice to everyone.

But my mother didn't know where I went when I headed out for walks, just as she didn't know that my best friend these days lived in a barn or that Wayne Johnson had admitted in an earlier note that he sometimes sat on our front steps at night, listening for the sound of my voice through the door. I groaned out loud. If only I'd found the notes myself, I would have told Wayne to his face that he was gross and he would have whined an apology, and everything would have been fine.

I stood, tossed the twig into the stream, and turned around.

Here the romance story asserts itself again, the way romance stories often do, against our will. Because I wasn't alone in the woods. My sorrowful performance hadn't been wasted on the trees. At the top of the hill, leaning against a naked birch with his hands stuffed into the pockets of his jeans stood a boy, backlit by the setting sun and hazy around the edges. With his shoulder-length hair and button-down shirt billowing in the breeze, he looked like the cover of a paperback novel. I couldn't see his face clearly, but his body language was relaxed and confident, defiant even, as he stood on our property.

An electric shock went through my body, transporting me out of this raggedy life and into a grand scenario, a world in which violins could start playing in the background and maybe the boy next door would turn out to be a hero after all. But only for a moment, because it was still Wayne Johnson standing on the hillside, spitting, freezing cold Wayne who had been the only one who knew where I was. I walked toward him up the hill, anger bubbling again, and near the top I glanced at him, ready to let loose, but he wasn't laughing at me, wasn't grinning or frowning, didn't look sorry or sad. He was just watching. As I neared, he lifted his eyebrows the slightest bit, a question, then stepped off the trail to let me pass, and in that courtesy, that stepping aside, I sensed danger for the first time.

A smile threatened my lips, but I managed to turn it into a scowl and to ask, "What are you looking at?" in a tone that didn't require an answer. Then I broke into a jog, down the other side of the hill toward a home that wasn't home, feeling flattered and sorry and above all confused because someone had come looking for me, someone did care.

I sped up, eager to get to the house, to slip through the back door and down into the basement where the last load of laundry would be dry by now. I wanted to fold towels and tee shirts, to match socks and make piles of underwear, creating order out of chaos until the day, the week, the year made some kind of sense. Until the question stopped rattling in my brain: what about Wayne? What, what, what about Wayne?

ARS ROMANTICA
(OR A DOZEN WAYS OF
LOOKING AT LOVE)

I. Geometrically

According to Robert Sternberg, the psychology researcher who developed the triangle theory of love, this emotion works the way colors do. The triangle's three points are intimacy, passion, and commitment, and its sides represent their combinations, so just as yellow mixed with red makes orange, intimacy and passion make *romance.* Just as red mixed with blue makes purple, intimacy and commitment make *companionable love.* And just as blue mixed with yellow makes green, commitment and passion make *foolish love.*

I don't mean to oversimplify. There are shades and nuances to love, the emotional equivalents of periwinkle and burnt umber, along with additional triangles that map the real and the ideal, the past and the future, the feelings and the behaviors they spark. But it's the sparks themselves that interest me most, the winks and compli-

63

ments, the moist palms, the constant, low-grade pleasure of attraction.

Ben Bishop was a retired art professor who owned the house I shared with one man during the time I was seeing a second. The second man knew about the first, but not the other way around, and Ben Bishop knew about everything but didn't mention it. We talked instead of our work, our travels. I had recently moved back to New York State from a year in Spain, which interested Ben because he'd once spent a summer with a woman in Málaga. The way his voice softened as he said this, eyebrows wrinkling above black-framed glasses, told me it had been an unspeakable time, happy and sad, thrilling and dangerous. We became fast friends.

In restaurants I noticed others noticing us, Ben's white hair and mustache, my unwrinkled skin, our cocktails and laughter. And how could I fault their conclusions? We *were* dating, Ben and me, all through that fall and into the winter, a period of brilliant colors fading to shadows and light.

II. Artistically

Ben lived at the end of a long driveway, in a ramshackle house filled with riches. He'd been a painter all his life, until macular degeneration began to erase detail. Now he sculpted in a workshop off the living room, where tables and shelves held large clay images. A life-sized hawk spread its wings, each feather responding to the wind. A curious child bent over a patch of grass. A three-foot-high bull with angular muscles and fearsome genitalia stood guard.

I lived next door, in a blue house with pink shutters. It was a fairy-tale house, backed into a steep, wooded hillside, with many small rooms and a set of stairs so narrow we had to sidestep up and down. The man I lived with had moved into the house while I was in Spain, as he finished the master's degree program where we'd met. Now, unable to find work in the Hudson Valley, he commuted to Long Island during the week and returned home each weekend. In contrast, I kept to a small local radius. Twice a week I drove over the mountain to teach classes at the university, a nine-mile route both beautiful and harrowing. On the other days I stayed at home, writing in a closet-sized room overlooking the stream out front.

On my home days Ben sometimes called in the late afternoon, his voice gruff with the day's silence: "Got anything in your fridge, sweetheart?" He might have leftover lasagna and three oranges, to which I'd add the makings of a salad and a bottle of wine. We'd agree to meet at his place at six, and from the moment I hung up the phone, the day shimmered. Loneliness evaporated, buoyancy took over. The last hour of work was the most productive of all.

The walls of Ben's house were crowded with paintings, charcoal drawings, pencil and ink sketches. Most were gifts from friends around the world, artists who lived by their talents and gave plenty away. On each visit, Ben and I chatted through the rooms, the studio with its cool clay scent, the living room with layers of handmade rugs, the kitchen bursting with color: yellow walls, red cabinets, exposed pipes painted blue and green. Everywhere I looked were images worth lingering in front of, and Ben was always happy to lead a tour. In the dining room we talked about the shading of a portrait at eye level; on the stairway we leaned against the railing, admiring the work of a collage artist. Upstairs in Ben's bedroom, shelves beside the window held abstract rosewood sculptures so smooth I couldn't help touching them. Mosquito netting curtained the unmade bed, as if we lived in Zanzibar.

Before dinner we'd have two, maybe three martinis, then switch to whatever wine I'd brought, and later there would be a nightcap of brandy or cognac, more than I could drink in an evening before or since. Ben's gruff exterior softened with each pour, though he never seemed drunk and I never felt that way. I felt charged up, connected to something I couldn't name. Ben asked questions and listened to the answers, both of us musing about books and movies and why people act the way they do. After we'd washed and dried the dishes and divided the leftovers, he'd walk me to the door and say, "That was a good time, sweetheart. Let's do it again."

The walk home, from the reach of Ben's porch light through darkness to the reach of my porch light, felt magical. Partly it was the drinks and the way Ben conversed as if my life experience were on par with his, but mostly it was the studio, the walls, the sculptures and paintings and sketches, the intimacy of all that expression. This was years before researchers at the University of London learned that looking at an appealing work of art stimulates the same areas of the brain as having a crush on a person, years before I began to understand why I'd float home from Ben's house feeling dizzy in love. I'd make a cup of tea and wrap in a blanket, then sit on the porch and look at the stars. Even when the temperature fell below freezing, I wanted to be out in the world, inhaling deeply, enjoying all that craving.

III. Platonically

When we talk about a platonic relationship, we mean no sex. No romance. Nothing untoward going on. But in Plato's *Symposium,* erotic love isn't only physical. Diotima, the wise woman who teaches Socrates about love, explains to him that there are two kinds of Eros: one centered in the body, the other in the mind.

Ben and I saw little of each other on weekends. Most Saturday evenings I went to the movies with the man who was back from Long Island or we hosted dinner parties for friends who barreled over the mountain with guitars and baklava. He did most of the cooking, and I lit candles, poured wine, washed dishes between courses because we didn't have enough plates. He called me "Sweetie" and rubbed my back, just as he always had, and the candles, the music, the lively conversation squeezed around a table in the living room made my heart race.

Some weekends Ben visited his girlfriend, also a retired teacher, in Brooklyn, or they traveled together to Taos or Marin County, or sometimes she came up and they hosted their own parties. I liked her and she seemed to like me, just as Ben liked the man I lived with. Sunday afternoon might find us all chatting in the driveway, noting how fast or slow the stream was running, how hunting season was about to start and good luck to our deer, but beyond that, we didn't socialize. Then when everyone else was gone and the workweek underway, Ben would call and ask what was in my fridge. If the answer was not much, we'd take his car, with me driving so he could have an extra drink, and head into town. We weren't sneaking. We weren't keeping it a secret. But we liked to be alone together, to feel the energy around our table, to bask in the pleasure of connection.

Ben and I didn't talk about ideas, at least not in the outward, philosophizing way of Plato, but there were anecdotes that worked like allegories, stories that made us go still. Narrowed eyes, a slight nod, and we each existed in two places at once: in the restaurant and in some corner of memory shadowed by beauty or truth or pain. Or maybe we existed in three places, because the past is always connected to the future, especially when the future is uncertain. We came together and stepped apart, over and over again, our dates always ending before we ran out of things to say.

Were these conversations erotic? I want to say yes, of course, they were intellectually erotic. But isn't the intellect physical, too? Doesn't it live in the body? Didn't my skin tingle as we talked, and didn't my organs seem to enlarge until I could hardly sit still? The distinction Diotima makes between physical and intellectual eroticism matters, but change the angle slightly and it's harder to see.

My favorite part of Diotima's lesson comes not when she defines the erotic but when she corrects Socrates' simplistic understanding of love. He believes the god of love to be mighty, good, and just, but love is not a god, Diotima insists. It's a spirit who mediates between the world of men and the world of gods. Love is the in-between, the back-and-forth, the translator, the ferryman. Love is the fulcrum on which the teeter-totter rests, the enabler of stomach-churning, mind-spinning excitement, as well as the excitement itself, as well as the ever-present danger of falling to the ground. Must we expect it to be moral, too?

IV. Biologically

The new guy showed up at a mid-week cocktail party near campus. He was tall and broad, with curly black hair and a beard trimmed enough to show dimples. When I caught him looking at me, he flushed without turning away, then navigated the crowd and touched my upper arm. "I've heard about you," he said, squinting as though he'd been warned.

In another year, his intensity might not have appealed to me, but during that restless period, suspended between the everyday excitement of living abroad and the promise of beginning a doctoral program the following fall, I felt eager for something. Maybe him, I thought casually, as he cocked his head toward me, listening. He wanted to know what kind of work I was doing, besides the teaching, and I described a large, freelance writing project. He offered to help, which I did not think was a good idea (who was he, anyway?), but I accepted his invitation to meet for a drink the next afternoon to discuss it.

No sooner had I left the party than a biological urge began to build, and not the one that comes first to mind. It wasn't caused by testosterone, the hormone associated with physical desire even in women, but by dopamine and norepinephrine, the love hormones. How do I know this? Because by the time I saw him again the next day, I'd become preoccupied, imagining in great detail this man's life and personality and past and future, engaging in what Virginia Woolf called the illusion of romantic love, "a story one makes up in one's own mind about another person." I'd spent most of my workday staring out the window, watching the stream, falling behind and growing irritated because of it. Not that it was my fault, exactly. We don't often have control over attraction.

That's because of the biochemical reactions that take place, as revealed in MRI studies of the brain. Dopamine lights us up, makes us receptive, creates a feedback loop. Sitting on a barstool with his flannelled arm brushing against mine, I already wanted more—not of him, necessarily, but of the feeling of promise. Once dopamine floods the brain, the receptors that capture it grow, and if no deal-breaker shuts down the process, the craving only intensifies. You can try to talk yourself out of it, you can resist out of loyalty or ethics, but the brain won't cooperate. The brain is gearing up for more of that euphoric drug, reacting to potential romance as if it were cocaine.

Meanwhile, norepinephrine makes the heart race, increases anxiety, disrupts sleep. Biological anthropologist Helen Fisher notes that people around the world report these symptoms during the giddy stage of attraction, including the elderly and children as young as four. The urge for romance, Fisher maintains, is more primal than the urge for sex. In fact, many researchers today don't classify romantic love as an emotion. It's a motivation, they say, akin to hunger or thirst.

I didn't know any of this then, but even if I had, what difference would it have made? I still would have met the new guy at the bar, talked for ninety minutes, given him my phone number. And I still would have gotten into my car afterwards and driven out of town to Mountain Rest Road, where I stepped hard on the gas, scolding myself out loud. No way. Forget about him. Halfway up I would have downshifted to third, then to second on the switchbacks, holding my breath at the top as the road narrowed to one lane, dipped under a railroad trestle, and the mountain fell away, revealing the purple Catskills spread against a darkening sky. Then I would have popped into neutral and hung on tight, my foot hovering over the brake pedal as the car sped through the curves, forty, fifty, sixty miles an hour into the long stretch, and if my nerves held up I'd make it all the way without braking, sixty-eight, seventy miles an hour, hugging tight into the final curve before coasting the last half-mile to the driveway and checking, as always, for a light in Ben's studio.

V. Linguistically

In Spanish, love is more nuanced than it is in English. You don't love a person (*te quiero*) with the same verb you love, say, a pineapple (*me encanta*). In both Spanish and English, we can *fall* in love, echoing lost paradise and a lot of work ahead, but in Spanish the more common phrase carries a reflexive twist: *me enamoré de*. It's the grammatical equivalent of "Now I lay me down to sleep," with a subtle implication of agency, of choice. *I became in love.*

After completing a master's degree the previous year, I had moved to Spain to teach English, despite being in love with the man I now lived with. We'd been together for two years at that point, and we stayed together, emotionally speaking, during most of my time away. He visited for the winter holidays, when our reunion had all the dopamine and testosterone of a new beginning, and then in April he convinced me to spend Easter with him in the house he'd rented from Ben. He even bought my plane ticket home because, it turned out, he wanted to tell me in person that he'd been having an affair. A love affair, we call it, even when love is beside the point.

How much easier it would be if there were no agency, if we were all just the sum of our biological systems. But there are choices, all along the way. To meet for a drink, to meet again for lunch, to say yes when he offers to drive over the mountain to pick up some of my freelance materials to work on. To have dinner with the new guy on Wednesday and Ben on Thursday and spend the weekend with the man I lived with. To think hard about revenge and decide that isn't it. To keep secrets that could be justified, in theory, but that in practice are what they are.

The verb *to love* means so very many things. I loved the blue house with pink shutters and the wooden footbridge over the stream and the drive to and from work. I loved the valley in what felt like a spiritual way. And I loved, very much, the man I continued to live with. The word *love*, even when we qualify it with "romantic," does and does not describe. It circumscribes, draws a circle around, or an oval or a downward spiral. Or maybe it's more like a Venn diagram, red on one side, purple on the other, the area of overlap as thick as blood.

VI. Obsessively

Romantic love makes us crazy, we all know that. "A madness most discrete / A choking gall and a preserving sweet," wrote Shakespeare.

Images of the new guy came to me day and night, prompting fantasies, imaginary situations, dialogue both cool and sexy. Intrusive thinking, it's called, when your mind feels hijacked by romantic potential. But it wasn't only the new guy I thought too much about. There was also Ben, who occupied my mind far more than seemed reasonable. I often wondered what he was doing, hoped he might call, and strategized about whether it was too soon after our last date to call him. If I glanced out the window and saw his German shepherd, Duke, sniffing along the stream, I'd go out and check the mail, knowing that wherever Duke went, Ben was close behind. Before each of our dinners, I felt nervous and self-conscious, changing clothes several times, putting on a touch of mascara and lip gloss. I didn't want a physical relationship with Ben, but I wanted, very much, to be a woman worthy of him.

Then again, I thought often of the man I lived with. He called most nights from his parents' house, where he stayed while working for his brother's construction company. To look at him, you'd never have thought he could frame out walls and hang sheetrock. He was tall and thin, with delicate hands and a way of standing with one hip cocked that drew women to him. When he arrived home on Friday, dusty and tired, his green eyes shining, I'd have dinner in the oven, timed to when he got out of the shower, and we'd eat, talk, drink wine, fall into bed early. He woke before dawn even on weekends and would go downstairs and read until the floorboards above creaked under my weight. Then he'd start a pan of oatmeal and heat milk for my coffee. Every weekend morning I came downstairs to the smell of warm cinnamon.

What I'm trying to say is that all that fall and winter I felt in love. Completely, obsessively in love. And also heartbroken. And also, at times, crazy. Wasn't it Nietzsche who said, "There is always some madness in love, but there is also always some reason in madness"?

VII. Narratively

Along with his triangle theory of love, Robert Sternberg developed a theory to explain how the triangles form.

Throughout our lives we read and hear and watch stories that influence the way we think of love, and often without realizing it, we enact them. For some, love is a game or sport in which two sides square off. For some it's a mystery or a rescue fantasy or even a recipe with ingredients. And for some, the moral of the story is: love conquers all.

That's the narrative I'd clung to before moving to Spain. Love, if strong and stubborn enough, will conquer the difficulties in a relationship, even when those difficulties are compounded by time and distance. It will allow one person to go away for a year and the other to visit her, then go back home and find a house where the two of them will live together at the end of their separation.

That seemed a good plan, until he brought me back from Spain to confess the affair, the former bothering me more than the latter. Why hadn't he told me by phone? Because, he said, he was afraid I wouldn't come back at all. That was a coward's stance, and because of it I knew the future I'd expected wouldn't happen. But a couple months after I returned from Spain, the man invited me to the blue house for dinner. On a gorgeous summer evening, under a sky swirled rose and orange, we sat in rocking chairs on the front porch, listening to tree frogs and watching hummingbirds sip from jimsonweed beside the stream. The air smelled like wood mulch and cut grass, like something I wanted to roll around in, and all of it, the place and the air and the guy were too much to withstand. I agreed to move in, just for a while, just to see. Then the phone rang, and I could tell by the tone of his voice it was the woman he claimed not to have seen in months.

I left in a huff, vowing as I drove over the mountain that this was the end. And it would have been if he lived in a bland apartment complex in town. But by then I wanted the house. I wanted the air and the deer, the everyday beauty. I wanted whatever version of my future might begin there.

When I made the decision to go ahead and move in, I told myself I'd live in the blue house for this interim year, then make a clean break. I told that to the man I was moving in with, too, and he said it sounded like a fine idea. "Just for a year," he said, shrugging. "Then off you go." But before long he started joking about coming with me, about settling in Iowa City, about walking me to class before heading to work as a carpenter. "One day we'll look back on this period and laugh," he said.

"From different time zones," I scoffed, but I didn't trust myself to make it so.

One night as I drifted off to sleep, an image formed of the new guy, picking me up out of bed and carrying me down the narrow stairs and out the front door. A knight in a soft flannel shirt.

VIII. Secretly

Behavioral psychologist Dorothy Tennov coined the term "limerence" for the obsessive stage of infatuation, that period spent pining and desiring before a relationship begins. I wonder what we should call its opposite: a love affair in decline, with two people orbiting each other, held together by a past without a future.

Defatuation?

Illimerence?

On Christmas Day, we had dinner at my father's house followed by dessert at my mother's, all of us on our best behavior because holidays have a way of opening old wounds. Then we drove back over the mountain to an evening of reading and listening to music. Most of our friends were away, and Ben's house stood dark. In the dim light of our small rooms, we began to plan a New Year's Eve party for the following weekend. I wrote down the guest list he dictated, which included the new guy who was supposed to be helping with my freelance writing project. "Your partner," he called him, without irony.

On New Year's Eve, the new guy paid respectful attention to me until the stroke of midnight, when he made such a point of avoiding me during the round of hugs and kisses that a friend called the next day to ask if we were having an affair. "Not that I'd mind," she said. "In fact, I'd approve. I just want to know what's going on."

I told her that things were messy enough in my life, thank you very much. I didn't say that the new guy had been the last to leave the party, or that long after the man I lived with went to bed, we sat on the couch and talked, my legs stretched across his knees, his thumb lightly grazing the flesh above my sock.

During the week, when I had the house to myself again, the new guy drove over the mountain in a snowstorm. He arrived mid-afternoon, stayed for dinner, and by the time he was dressed and ready to leave at midnight, ten inches of snow lay on the unplowed roads. That's how Ben found out. Around lunchtime the next day, with six more inches of snow on the ground, the new guy and I trudged down the driveway to see what the road looked like. On the way back we met Duke and, not far behind, Ben. "What a day!" he called from under the furry hood of a parka. "Isn't it glorious?"

I introduced them, and Ben said to the new guy, "Got stuck last night, did you? There's a truck coming to plow, but who knows what time it'll get here." Then Ben turned to me, blinking behind those black-framed glasses, the corners of his mouth turned up just enough to tease me. "Need a shovel?"

"Nope," I said, meeting his gaze and holding it. "Is there anything you need?"

Ben smiled, reached an arm around my shoulder, and squeezed. "Not a thing, sweetheart. Not a thing."

IX. Mythologically

Ovid's *Metamorphoses* is filled with love stories, almost none of which turn out well. Male gods fall hard for women or nymphs or lesser goddesses, sometimes pursuing them to the point of rape, after which a kind god, or a jealous goddess, transforms them into birds or animals or trees. Often the state of being in love is a punishment, as when Apollo speaks condescendingly to Cupid and the boy-god retaliates with an arrow that makes Apollo immediately fall in love with Daphne, so in love that he harasses her until she convinces her father to turn her into a laurel tree.

But women, too, are prone to intense, even irrational desire in Ovid's world. In *The Art of Love*, he recounts the infatuation of Pasiphae, wife of Minos, for a white bull. Pasiphae handpicks sweet grass for the animal, has the most attractive of her heifer-rivals slaughtered, and eventually climbs inside a wooden cow built for the occasion, in order to present herself to the bull. The result of their union is the hybrid Minotaur.

Often in these tales desire has a single end, and once it's achieved the story moves on. But what about Pasiphae in the days and weeks after she mated with the bull? Did she feel satisfied? Debased by her animal instincts? Humiliated by her position inside the wooden cow, waiting for the bull to mount her? In the aftermath of consummation, did she return to the field?

After the snowstorm, I avoided the new guy. On the phone he sounded confused by my suddenly busy schedule, which included dinners and movies with friends and, of course, a weekend with the man who shared the blue house. If that man had grown suspicious, if he'd confronted me, I would have argued that our relationship was undefined now, that I was free to do as I pleased, including right there in the house where I lived. But I wouldn't have believed my own words.

Even so, it wasn't guilt or shame that made me recoil from the new guy. Before we slept together, I'd been almost deliriously attracted to him. His beard was soft, his hands broad and sure. His neck smelled like a cool, dark room on a sunny day. His desire for me had been constant, powerful, and tempered by bouts of shyness that made my lower back hum. But on that snowy night, after we'd chopped vegetables and put the soup to simmer, after we'd looked each other in the eye and gone upstairs, I felt the way Pasiphae might have. What real bull could match all that effort, the commissioning of a disguise, the justifications that must have made her actions seem inevitable? In bed, the new guy had been hesitant. Deferential, even. And who, I thought after he'd left, who in holy hell wants that?

X. Self-servingly

In January, Ben and Duke headed to Vermont for a few days, during which time I thought about going into Ben's house. He'd given me a key once when I'd taken care of Duke, then told me to hang onto it just in case. I didn't want to snoop; I just wanted to sit in the kitchen and absorb its colors, visit the charcoal drawing with the plump and pointed lines, go into the studio and run my hands along the back of that hyper-masculine bull. But finding no excuse to trespass, I stayed home, looking down the driveway ten times each day to see if they were back yet.

On Friday I had meetings all afternoon, and when I got home the man I lived with was already there, tucked into a bowl of minestrone soup he'd found in the back of the fridge. I told him it was the new guy's recipe, that he and I had made it the week before. "It's kind of old now."

"No, it's delicious," he replied, getting up to ladle a second bowl. "Want some?"

All weekend I looked for signs that he suspected my affair or that he'd grown detached enough not to mind. We went to the movies on Saturday night and for a hike on Sunday morning, then met friends for lunch before he left again for the week. No one, it seemed, sensed that anything was different.

Except me. Life was very different from the way I'd imagined it would be a year before. I hadn't necessarily expected the man to be faithful during my time in Spain, but I believed in, and we had discussed, the importance of honesty during that long-distance period. Now, whenever I thought about flying back from Spain the previous spring, how he picked me up at the airport looking happy and smitten and we made love that night and again the next day and not until the day after that, when he feared someone else might tell me, did he explain that he'd been sleeping with another woman, I wanted to pack my bags and move. But then Sunday afternoon arrived and he was gone, and I had the blue house to myself and, eventually, the burden of deciding whether I now owed the man I lived with the honesty I'd once expected of him.

Ben called on Monday morning. "Got home late last night and I'm ready to cook. What's your pleasure, sweetheart? Vegetarian chili? Quiche?"

I asked what the occasion was, and he replied, "I've missed you. Come over around six."

Outside the living room window, a gnarled branch had fallen from the apple tree and landed beside the driveway, where the snow gave it a rippled effect. A thick layer of ice coated the edges of the stream, while in the middle water glided over rocks worn round and smooth. Everything was white, black, gray, the subtle, beautiful palette of a new year.

I told Ben I'd love to spend the evening with him, but I already had plans.

"With who?" he asked, as if we were best friends or relatives or every bit as intimate as I'd begun to feel.

"A guy. You met him the day of the snowstorm."

There was a moment's pause before Ben said, "Oh, *him*. Just bring him with you. I'll make the chili."

When the new guy knocked on the back door, I was stirring a bowl of chocolate frosting. He took his boots off in the mudroom and hung his coat over the kitchen chair, then kissed my cheek and asked if there were anything he could do. I put him to work removing cupcakes from a pan, which helped the awkwardness.

He smelled clean, like gentle soap and a hint of clove. He'd brought a bottle of very nice wine for Ben. He told a funny story about a scene he'd witnessed in the grocery store. Most importantly, he kept his distance, so that by the time we were ready to head next door, I could imagine getting close to him again.

Before we left, I warned the new guy about Ben. "He's a character," I said. "He tells it like it is, no filter, and his house will knock you over." This was the same warning

I'd gotten in the summer, from the man I was about to live with, before we had dinner with Ben the first time. Don't be intimidated, he'd told me, but when we walked in and Ben greeted us, in his black jeans and white linen shirt, bare feet slapping against the slate floor, I felt myself shrink. What saved me was the feeling of intimidation itself, still so familiar from Spain where I'd had to hold my own despite feeling out of place every day, and which caused a mental adrenaline surge. In Ben's house, in his presence, I became a better conversationalist than I really was, if only for a few hours.

The opposite happened with the new guy. Despite my warnings that Ben's a character, a straight shooter, that his house will knock you over, the new guy got knocked over. Hard. In the studio, he raised his eyebrows and laughed at the sight of the bull. In the kitchen, he likened the colors to a kindergarten classroom. In front of a bright painting of our valley in autumn, he said, "Ah, influenced by the Hudson River school." I watched as Ben's face screwed up, saw the shake of his head, and fought the urge to step in and guide the conversation, because I knew he would think less of me for doing so.

In the doorway to Ben's bedroom, the view of rumpled white sheets and mosquito netting stripped the last of the new guy's composure. "And here's the *boudoir*," he sang as if trying not to be angry, and while I processed that, Ben responded in the even tone of voice he'd have used for the weather. "You really are an asshole, aren't you?"

For three, perhaps four seconds, my mind vacillated between horror and awe. What a terrible thing to say to a guest in your home! And what an impressive thing to say to anyone, especially with such composure! I wanted to laugh, partly out of discomfort and partly out of genuine amusement, but I stayed quiet instead, waiting. The man I lived with would have loved this story, if only there were a way to tell it to him.

The new guy shrugged and laughed. Over dinner, he seemed chastened yet dignified, more dignified than I could have been in his place, and that, together with the atmosphere of Ben's home, made me soften toward him again. But there was no winning Ben over. After dessert, after the nightcap, after Ben and I had divided the left-overs and done the dishes with no help from my date, Ben walked us to the door. "Well, it was nice knowing you," he said drily, extending his hand toward the new guy and giving me a wink that said we'd laugh about this next time.

In fact, the evening had changed things for me, although not in the way Ben assumed.

His candor that evening made me see how dishonestly I lived in the fairy-tale house, behaving as if a happy ending were possible with the man I still loved. But it wasn't possible, and this carrying on with the new guy was evidence of that. I needed to move.

I could see that the new guy wasn't someone who would be in my life for long, but he would offer encouragement and help stave off loneliness, and without him, I wasn't sure I'd go through with the separation. This, too, was dishonest, continuing a new relationship in order to end an old one, but sometimes the triangle theory of love doesn't work the way it should. Sometimes intimacy plus passion doesn't equal romance. Sometimes it equals calculation, a self-serving means to a necessary end.

XI. Ironically

The man I lived with showed up unannounced on a Thursday evening. He'd finished a job that afternoon and decided to take a long weekend, driving upstate through pouring rain that hadn't dampened his spirits.

It could have been the classic, "I came home and found my girlfriend in bed with another man," but as it happened, the new guy had stayed over the night before, gone home in the morning, and just returned with the freelance materials he'd insisted on helping me with but had never actually opened. I couldn't have scripted a more innocent scene: the new guy still wore his coat and held a manila envelope, which he delivered with apologies. The man I lived with shook the new guy's hand and gave me a kiss and, delighted with the three-day weekend ahead, suggested we all go out for drinks. "I'll drive," he said.

Outside we discovered that, because the new guy's car was blocking the driveway, the man I lived with had parked off to the side in such a way that one front tire sunk into a patch of mud. "Oh well," he said. "Good thing we've got two more cars to choose from."

The new guy offered to drive but insisted we get the other car out first, while he was there to help. As I stepped on the gas and they pushed, the front tire sank farther. Then I had a brainstorm. I dug some of the mud away from the stuck tire and wedged rocks and small branches behind it. When everything was in place, I stood beside the car, shouting instructions. "Turn left! A little more! Now reverse and gun it!" The wheel caught and spun, the car lurched back, and I had time for a single heartbeat of pride at my own engineering before a fountain of mud arced into the air and, like a choreographed comeuppance, rained onto my face. As I stood there, a cartoon character left holding the fuse of an exploded bomb, my biggest concern was that Ben might step outside at just that moment and witness poetic justice.

Two days later I paid the deposit for a small attic apartment. When I broke the news to the man I lived with, he nodded sadly and went upstairs to bed. Half an hour later he came down again, having finally put everything together. "How could you?" he gasped. "We were doing so well! Everything was great until he came along!"

XII. Metaphysically

In his "Definition of Love," seventeenth-century poet Andrew Marvell describes a romance so perfect it approaches the divine, prompting jealous fate to intervene so the lovers remain like two parallel lines, appearing to approach one another but never actually touching. It's a love without hope, the child of despair and impossibility.

What color would that kind of love be? What shape would depict it best?

I'd met the man I lived with in a seventeenth-century literature course. After class we sometimes went to a bar where we drank bourbon and pored over the textbook, deciphering poems for the pleasure of saying the lines aloud and puzzling out their cryptic meanings. I'd never experienced anything like it. The man was handsome and smart and unabashed about loving literature, and I fell in love with the way his mind took hold of mine.

Three years later, when things went bad between us, it felt like the cosmos opposed our union. And yet I moved in anyway, refusing to accept the inevitable even as I knew this deep love was doomed.

Ben was the consolation prize. His friendship, with its romantic undertones, its deep appreciations, allowed me to imagine a greater purpose in the transition time. His sweet property, the houses and the stream and the scent of wood smoke in the air, along with being let into his home for brief glimpses of an artistic life, showed me what was possible. There is little I've wanted to do less in my life than move away from him.

Out in the driveway on a mild February morning, Duke sniffed circles around us as I told Ben about the new apartment. "I can't keep living with him," I explained.

Ben nodded, frowning. "You realize that once you're gone, he'll leave, too."

I did realize that, but the man I lived with held the lease. Neither Ben nor I could make him move.

An hour later, my phone rang. Ben explained that he'd been meaning to spend more time in Brooklyn and might head down there for a month or two. Why didn't I house-sit for him? He wouldn't charge me a cent, and once the man next door saw I wasn't coming back to him, he'd move out and I could have the blue house.

I imagined waking up in Ben's bed, underneath the mosquito netting, diffuse sunlight coming through the north windows. I imagined drinking coffee in his kitch-en and stretching out on his couch, pretending I'd earned those surroundings, the fruits of an incessantly produc-tive life. How I would have loved that. But I knew that the man I lived with, who'd become morose and accusato-ry as I packed, was not going to move out with me living next door, and anyway, I didn't trust myself to keep such a short distance from him. In order to leave that relation-ship, I had to leave Ben, too.

I also knew this: Ben and I adored each other, and that was fine when we were neighbors. But soon, once we could no longer chat in the driveway or do small favors for each other, our casual, shimmering friendship would end. Even if we got together now and then for dinner or martinis, the homey intimacy would be gone. I didn't want to be part of Ben's social circle, someone with whom he made plans in advance. I wanted to be the person he called on a lonely Tuesday afternoon, the kindred spirit to whom he offered a drink at the end of a day spent shaping details around the darkening center of his vision. I wanted to be the person he called when his car wouldn't start and he needed to catch the bus to Manhattan, the person who would throw a coat on over her pajamas and drive him to town, marveling at how lightly he traveled, how easily he joked, how much he seemed like a young man living in an aged man's body. I wanted what we'd had and wouldn't be able to sustain.

After I moved, things played out as expected. The man I'd lived with broke the lease and left the area. Meanwhile, the new guy proclaimed his feelings for me and grew angry when I didn't reciprocate. "What does love mean to you, anyway?" he demanded. I tried to explain the difference between infatuation and a bond that takes time to form, the difference between early, obsessive excitement and a deep sense of connection, of security. But all the while I was thinking of Ben, of how to characterize what I felt for him, which was neither of those things and which I experienced during the weeks and months after I moved as the purest form of loss.

That spring I bought a gift for Ben, a box of imported Italian cookies, and drove over the mountain several times hoping to find him home. His car was never in the driveway, and eventually I ate the cookies myself in a fit of angry sorrow as I packed for Iowa. I told myself that the following summer, when I came back to visit, I would make sure to see him.

But during my first winter away, a snowstorm blew into the Hudson Valley so suddenly and with such force that Ben didn't even try the mountain pass before taking a safer route ten miles out of the way. He and his girlfriend were coming home from dinner, and not far from the house the car slid off the road into a tree. "I'm so sorry," the friend who called to tell me kept saying, as I imagined the snow, the headlights and shadows, the skid, the impact, the cold, white silence.

More than once since then, on trips to the Hudson Valley, I've driven up and over the mountain, down through the curves, slowing to a crawl as the road snakes past the mailboxes and the stream and the two houses nestled like old friends or pseudo-lovers or companionable ghosts. Each time my chest swells with anticipation, palms begin to sweat, the car slows almost to a stop, and for a moment time and space seem to warp, the past becoming present and the present receding into the future, like two parallel lines—or three or four—angled imperceptibly toward one another. "Magnanimous despair," Marvell called it. The color of clay.

BOY CRAZY

Buzz-cut hair. Tee shirts tucked neatly into swim trunks. This was not a look that attracted Monica and me. During the summer before ninth grade, we preferred the messiness of rock stars: long tresses, bare feet, shorts that used to be pants. But the two guys across the boardwalk kept glancing our way, and we kept glancing back, watching the giant roulette wheel behind them spin and slow.

Behind us green waves slapped at a beach teeming with oiled bodies. In front of us the boardwalk stretched farther than we could see in either direction, its creosote smell brought out by the sun. Monica turned toward me, looking over her shoulder as if searching the beach for her parents, and I caught her tangy sweetness, a mix of Enjoli perfume, tanning oil, and grape bubble gum. "Coming up on the right," she said in a low voice. "Gray shorts. Hair like Steve Tyler." I crossed one leg over the other, ankle bracelet chiming, and scanned past him—great hair—and back again.

"Ladies?" said this gorgeous guy in cut-off sweats, with black belly hairs curling above his waistband.

"Sir?" Monica replied. His face melted, head tilted back as he laughed, and before he was far enough away we lost it.

Two years before, when Monica's parents first brought me along on their summer vacation, I felt gob-smacked by everything: the exit names on the Garden State Parkway (Ho-Ho-Kus, W Freehold, Brick Twp), the stillness of Barnegat Bay, the constant movement of the vast, powerful ocean. I loved the games of chance along the boardwalk, interspersed with ice cream stands and saltwater taffy shops, the amusement pier with its wooden roller coaster and loud rock music, the cable cars that stretched along the northern half of the boardwalk. Monica and I had ridden those cars several times a night, singing the whole way, giddy with the freedom of vacation and caring about only one thing: fun.

There's a lifetime between twelve and fourteen. This year I felt grown and responsible and not so easily impressed. That first vacation had happened soon after my parents reconciled, at a time when I was trying to fit back into my old life, and the break from the tension at home felt like paradise. Since then, my parents had split once more, and although I'd gone with my mother on the first round, I refused to move on the second. I lived with my father now but saw him only on weekends and during his half-hour supper break each weeknight. I'd have a meal on the table when he arrived at 6:35 p.m. and would clean up after he left just before 7:00 p.m. Apart from that, I spent the after-school hours as I saw fit—watching TV, practicing cartwheels in the living room, catching the bus downtown with Monica to shoplift makeup and talk about our next trip to Seaside Heights, New Jersey.

Monica stood up and turned to face the ocean. She was tall, with broad shoulders and hips, and as she undid the towel around her waist and rewrapped it low, around the bottom of her two-piece bathing suit, the buzz-cut guys across the boardwalk took notice.

"Heads up," I announced, turning to gaze out on the bodies and too-bright sand, on the ocean that moved so incessantly, advancing and drawing back again.

Instead of approaching, the guys sat on the next bench, playing it cool as if we hadn't noticed them noticing us. Up close I could see their acne and sunburn, but there were two of them at least and one was tall. I shook the foot with the bracelet a few times and ran my eyes past them, but they seemed to have chickened out. Or maybe they'd seen us up close and weren't interested anymore. After a couple minutes, Monica asked if was ready, and I lingered, stretched, reached into my pocket for some lip gloss. I'd been right to begin with: these two were not possibilities. Still. They could have offered a compliment or made a little joke.

Just as we began to walk away, one angled his head to catch my eye and said, "Nice day." I nodded, heart sinking, and waited until we were out of earshot before leaning into Monica. "What was he, like, fifteen?" I groaned. She shook her head sadly and tightened her lips as if exhaling smoke. This was vacation, a hundred tiny disappointments every day.

"Summertime, oh summertime, pattern of life indelible." That's E. B. White in "Once More to the Lake," capturing the nostalgia adults so often feel for the vacation terrain of our youth. My nostalgia is different, located firmly in the past, in the melancholic fourteen-year-old who feared that the best years might already be behind her. The purpose of vacation, in her mind, was to seek some sign or omen, some glimmer of hope for the future.

At night Monica and I walked the boardwalk, feeding off the energy of the crowd and the amplified guitar riffs, buzzers, bells. We rode the Log Flume and the roller coaster, played roulette and arcade pinball, eyes peeled all the while for a pair of attractive guys. Sometimes we'd stop to lean against the railing with our backs to the ocean, scanning the crowd. Monica might say, "Two benches down, I call the guy on the right," so I'd check out his friend on the left. We'd hatch a plan for getting their attention and then just before one of us made a move, here would come two teenage girls squeezing onto the bench between them. "Oh, fuck *me*," one of us would groan. Girlfriends.

In truth, the girls of the boardwalk captivated us as much as the boys. We watched them the way we watched ourselves, looking for flaws and admiring traces of beauty. Ten times a day Monica nudged me to look at a girl and said, "Great skin" or "That's the stomach I need" or, more often, "I want to look exactly like *her*." The girl was always tall and thin and had long hair, and if she was blonde I'd say, "You *do* look like her, stupid, just let your hair grow," and Monica would smack my arm, grinning.

The girls I admired shared an attitude more than a physical type. They seemed completely at home on the boardwalk, their bare feet impervious to the scorching boards and splinters. They met people's eyes without looking away, and when they caught me watching they'd sometimes smile or even say hello, making me blush. I couldn't imagine how to go from being someone like me to someone like them and wondered whether it really was true, as Monica always said, that wanting something long enough would make it happen.

In the midst of cruising the boardwalk, we took smoke breaks, indulging the habit we'd begun back in the spring in order to lose weight. That hadn't worked, but smoking gave a rhythm to the hours and days, so we kept our bags stocked with gum, our boxes of Newports zipped into secret compartments, and never smoked on the boardwalk where Monica's parents might see us. Instead we retreated to out-of-the-way benches behind hotels and restaurants, places where we could pretend to be grown women, enjoying life on our own.

By Thursday, the next-to-last full day of vacation, Monica and I were growing frantic. This was supposed to be the year we left our inexperienced, junior high selves behind, the year we broke out of our shells and stepped up to the plate and got some action. Not that we wanted a lot of action. We just wanted to connect, hold hands, make out under the stars. That was the whole purpose of going away, wasn't it? To store up experience and create memories that would shimmer all year, infusing regular life with a radiant glow.

That evening we put on our best outfits, Monica in a short skirt and nylon tee shirt, and me in gauzy white pants and a halter top. As we left the rental cottage, Monica's father whistled and told us to be careful, while her mother reminded us to be home by 11 p.m.

The boardwalk was just a few blocks away, and from the moment we stepped onto it, all kinds of guys offered compliments, but the only ones who stopped to talk were our parents' age. Then, just before sunset, a bench opened and we planted ourselves like a couple of flowering palms. It didn't take long to hear a whistle and glance toward its source, two guys strolling down the middle of the boardwalk, heads turned our way. We smiled and they veered toward us. "See? That's what I like," the one who had whistled called out, "a girl who appreciates a compliment!" He was maybe eighteen, short and stocky, waving his hands as he talked. Not someone I would normally gravitate toward, but his buddy was taller than Monica, which made them viable.

The whistler slapped his friend on the back. "See?" he called, "These girls understand that a whistle means, *you look good.*" His voice was loud, but his facial expression so genial I started to laugh. "These girls aren't like the other girls who get all pissed off when you whistle at them. There's nothing I hate more, man, than a pretty girl who can't take a compliment. You know what I mean?" He was talking directly to me now, grinning. "I can tell you girls are different. You're not like those stuck-up bitches."

Monica was smiling at the taller one like it was Christmas morning. The whistler kept talking about how nice we both looked, what a pretty picture we made with the ocean behind us and the stars just coming out, and then he asked what we were up to and before Monica could open her mouth, I said, "Waiting for our boyfriends," with just the right note of apology.

"Oh, you slay me," he said, crossing his hands over his chest dramatically. After another minute they said goodbye, and Monica turned to me, glaring and wanting to know what in the holy hell I was thinking.

I couldn't explain it, exactly, but the word "bitches" reverberated in my mind. How narrowly we'd escaped that label. If we hadn't heard the whistle or hadn't smiled, these guys might have continued down the boardwalk, cursing us. And would they have been justified? I wondered what kind of girls got upset at a guy's whistle. What bothered the bitches of the boardwalk?

I shrugged and said I didn't like the guys, and Monica wanted to know why not and so what and who died and left me with full veto power. "It's *Thursday*," she groaned, digging in her bag for the box of Newports. "Jesus, we are running out of time."

We got up and headed for our favorite smoking spot, out back of the pinball arcade beside a large saltwater pool. Not many people used the pool, which made sense since it was only half a block from the ocean, but just beyond it stood a four-story water slide. During the day we scoped out guys on the slide, then said hello to the cute ones when they dripped past.

At night there weren't many people back there, so we smoked in silence, Monica staring at the cement while I watched a couple soaking their feet in the shallow end of the pool. The sky above turned from purple to black, and I thought about the girls I admired on the boardwalk. Did they get offended when guys whistled at them? And if so, why? I wished I had someone to ask about this, an older sister or cousin, someone who understood how these things worked. I wished I could ask my mother, but since she moved out, I refused to talk to her about anything important.

Then Daniel appeared. Neither of us saw him coming; he just materialized, standing in front of our bench, smiling and saying "Hey," as if we were old friends. Dimples formed parentheses around his mouth, his eyes were deep blue, and even with the short hair beneath his backwards baseball cap he was rock-star gorgeous. I couldn't believe he was talking to us, let alone saying that he worked on the waterslide and had seen us sitting over here during the day in our bathing suits. I sized him up—

medium height, strong build, wearing a snug white tank top, faded Levis, red sneakers, no socks. If he had a tall friend, we were in business.

Monica sat with one long leg draped over the other, and Daniel's eyes kept dropping toward the hem of her skirt. He asked where we were from and how long we were staying, and she told him one more day. "Then we don't have much time," he said brightly. "How about a drink at The Wine Cellar?" I took a drag off my cigarette, pretending to think, while Monica responded in a voice so cool I hardly recognized it. "We'd love to, Daniel, but the problem is we're only seventeen. And you know the bouncer at The Wine Cellar, the really big guy? Last night he took our fake IDs."

Daniel laughed with delight. "Seventeen! Wow, you girls are mature for your age." Daniel was twenty-one, but he remembered seventeen like it was yesterday. "Not much changes after seventeen," he said. "By now, you girls pretty much know everything you need to know, right?"

"Pretty much," I said, and his eyes lingered for a long moment on mine.

In her essay "Goodbye to All That," Joan Didion describes her early adulthood in New York City with this poignant line: "I had never before understood what 'despair' meant, and I'm not sure that I understand now. But I understood that year." Rather than condescend to her younger self, Didion grants her a degree of knowledge she no longer possesses. I want to do the same, but what did I understand at fourteen? Not desperation so much as loneliness and the fear of being unworthy—of a family, a mother. But that isn't how I perceived things then.

Then, all I knew with certainty was that if vacation could make me feel desirable, then going home again on Saturday would be less crushing.

That's why I didn't hesitate when Daniel suggested we go back to his place. Neither did Monica, although we kept an eye out for her parents on the way. The apartment stood a block off the northern end of the boardwalk, in a house with several mailboxes out front. Daniel's door was tucked around the side and up a few steps, but his living room windows looked right onto the street. From inside we could clearly hear the conversations of people walking by, so I wasn't concerned when Daniel said, "You girls don't mind if I lock the door, right? I always keep the door locked, but there's nothing to worry about. You can trust me."

The paneled living room fit a loveseat, armchair, coffee table, and stereo. Monica and I sat down on the love seat and looked around at the brown shag carpet, the seascape hanging beside the door, the turntable and speakers on the floor below the window. The apartment wasn't much, but Daniel worked and paid rent and lived here without anyone to oversee him, which I found thrilling.

At the edge of the living room stood a kitchenette, with a half-sized refrigerator from which Daniel took three cans of Budweiser. Monica and I accepted the cans like it was no big deal, then pantomimed screaming when he turned his back. As Daniel lowered the needle onto the Rolling Stones' *Some Girls*, I watched the way he moved, the fluid bend of his body, how when he knelt on the floor, adjusting knobs, the waistband of his jeans bowed away from the soft cotton of his tank top. He kept the volume low, which I thought was a good sign.

"So," Daniel said, slouching into the chair and throwing one leg over its arm. "What's the story?"

The beer was very cold and I felt both mature and awkward sipping it in the apartment of a guy who had bought it legally. Monica asked how long Daniel had worked at the waterslide, and he shrugged. "Doesn't matter. It's just a shit job, man, who cares about that?" He wanted to talk about us, about who our friends were, what they looked like, what we had planned for our senior year of high school.

As we talked, Daniel relaxed. His eyelids grew heavy, his torso sank into the chair. I relaxed, too, slipping my feet out of my sandals and drawing one leg up under me. He asked about what we did at home on the weekends and about the guys we dated, and we riffed off each other, fabricating social lives.

When the beer cans were empty, Daniel asked if we wanted more, and we both said no thanks. He didn't press. Instead, he got up and stepped over my sandals, then wedged himself onto the loveseat between Monica and me. I scooted over as far as possible, but his hip rested against mine and his arms spread out around our shoulders. I felt the warmth of his cotton shirt, smelled the sweetly pungent scent of his underarm.

"Girls," he said, "I am feeling fine right now. How about you? Are you feeling as fine as I am?"

Monica snorted. "Oh, sure. I feel just great." Her sarcastic tone got no response, and I wondered about the change in Daniel after only one beer. He didn't seem drunk, but he wasn't sober either. He must have taken something just before he met us, and now it was kicking in.

"I like it that you girls trust me," Daniel cooed, rubbing my shoulder. "I like that you came back here to my apartment without knowing me. That's a good sign." His hand snaked awkwardly down my upper arm and hovered in front of my left breast. "You are good, good girls," he half whispered, and his tone felt like a rubber band snapping against my cheek. In an instant, I was up, feet in my sandals and moving toward the door, which I unlocked and opened in one quick motion. With a hand on the screen door I looked at the love seat. Daniel hadn't moved. His left arm still hung in the air, his right resting on Monica's shoulder. His face wore an expression of mild surprise.

"Thanks for the beer," I said, "but we're supposed to meet her parents at 11:00 and it's almost that time." Monica wriggled out from under his arm and stood.

Daniel stood, too, rocking side to side. "Don't tell me you really have to go." His voice took on a whine, his handsome eyes pleading. "Don't tell me you're going to leave me here all by myself. Come on, you're such beautiful girls."

I said, "Thanks, but Monica's father has a real temper. He's Italian."

This didn't faze Daniel. "Monica, sweetheart, stay here with me," he said, taking hold of her arm. "Let your friend go meet your parents and tell them you're busy. You're so pretty, Monica, come on. Please?" And then standing right there in front of me, he began to kiss her. Worse than that, she kissed him back.

I let the screen door slam behind me and stood on the top step. So often it felt like Monica and I were slightly different versions of the same person. We didn't look anything alike, and she was older by half a year, but we had so much in common that it didn't bother me when friends or teachers called us by each other's names. And it didn't really bother me now that it was Monica kissing Daniel. I knew it could just as easily have been me. In Daniel's mind the only difference between us was that one got to the door faster than the other. I was the party pooper and she was the daredevil. Fine, I thought. Just hurry up and let's get out of here.

On the street, someone was trying to parallel park a Buick, its rear wheel rolling onto the curb again and again. Surely, I thought, Monica and I deserved better than this. Where were all the cute, sweet teenaged guys who might appreciate us? Wouldn't someone appreciate us? Actually be interested in us? Did we really have to settle for guys like Daniel?

Behind me Daniel said, "Hold on, let me close this door." Monica replied, "No, leave it open," and Daniel insisted, "I want it closed."

Once again, my body acted on instinct, pulling the screen door open and planting my foot inside the threshold. "Monica, *come on*," I hissed. Daniel's baseball hat was off his head, his brown hair matted with its outline. Slowly his eyes focused on me. "What are you doing here?" he asked softly. "Your friend and I want to be alone. Don't be such a bitch."

I stepped inside and took Monica by the arm, pulling her toward the door. Daniel grabbed her other arm. "I'm not playing around," he said, eyes flashing. I expected Monica to wrench her arm free and follow me out the door, down the steps, up the street running. This guy was obviously messed up, high or deranged or both, so when Monica said, "Just wait outside for a few minutes, OK? We'll leave the door open," the wind went out of me.

The street outside was full of life, couples and groups walking past, to or from the boardwalk. Beyond the streetlights a few stars were visible, and the ocean breeze dried my skin as I paced, furious. We had an agreement to stick together, to look for guys in pairs and never let one come between us. This was pure selfishness on Monica's part, making us miss curfew. If her parents grounded us tomorrow night, our last night here, I would never forgive her.

I smoked two cigarettes, blowing smoke toward the window to remind Monica of my presence. Finally I crept back up the steps and peered through the screen door. They were still standing in front of the couch, kissing and swaying as if dancing, with Monica's arm moving at waist level, back and forth. I sat down on the top step, straining to hear the instructions he gave her—hold tighter, not so fast. In front of me, a couple walked arm in arm, his hand tucked into the back pocket of her shorts. Inside, Daniel's throat found something like a hum.

Afterwards, as we hurried down the street toward our cottage, Monica giggled an apology. She promised never to do anything like this again and told me not to worry, she'd handle her parents, but listen, I had to listen. It felt like a muscle, you know? A muscle this thick around and covered with soft skin, soft like you can't believe. The hair's kind of coarse and naturally she didn't get a good look or anything, but holy shit what a night!

I told Monica she was a terrible friend. That she owed me big time. Didn't she see how wasted that guy was? If not for me, she might be dead right now.

She stopped and grasped both my arms. "Thank you for not leaving," she said, before pulling me into a tight embrace. Then we both broke into a run.

On Friday I had sulking rights, which meant I could be as sarcastic and demanding as I wanted and Monica had to be nice back. But I wasn't really mad anymore. Throughout the day we retold the story of Daniel to each other: how reckless we'd been going to his apartment, how brave I was to stand up to him, how crazy that Monica's first time making out with a guy involved a hand job. And how totally cool that he believed we were seventeen. With each telling the story made me feel deeper and wiser, more substantial. In future years, I would think of this experience when Monica and I paired off with guys on a dark beach or climbed into souped-up cars headed for Point Pleasant, and for a long time, the best part of it all would be comparing notes afterwards, telling ourselves the stories that were shaping us.

On this last day of vacation, it was time to buy souvenirs. I got an ashtray for my father, a bag of saltwater taffy for my brother, matching tee shirts for Monica's parents to thank them for bringing me along. That left only my mother. In each store I looked at the same touristy gifts— conch shells, earrings in the shape of lobsters, shot glasses, decorative plates—but nothing seemed right. Then in the last possible shop, I spotted a series of wooden plaques carved into words. "Mom," "Seaside Heights," "I Love NJ," and one that especially caught my eye, its fat, cartoonish letters spelling "BITCH." Monica clasped her hand over her mouth at the sight of it, and I didn't know how to explain to her, or even to myself, that the word meant something new, something I wanted to know more about, something irreverent but also, potentially, admirable. In a nod toward everything I didn't yet know, I bought it, hoping my mother would understand.

That night we cruised the boardwalk, flirting with hysterical longing. If we could just find the right pair of guys, there was still time for one walk on the beach, one makeout session, one hour of romance. And then not. Monica cajoled me into a last ride on the roller coaster, after which we started the devastating walk back to the cottage, along the darker end of the boardwalk. Monica wept while I reminded her that this year *was* different, that at least *she*'d gotten a little action. But that didn't help either of us.

An empty bench beckoned, and although it meant we'd get home late again, we sat down facing the ocean. The breeze was warm and gentle, in rhythm with the waves. The moon, not quite full but getting there, cast a white streak along the water, and wispy clouds trailed across the sky. I listened to Monica's breathing, to her sniffles and sighs, and to the ocean, pushing and receding, breaking and gathering itself up again. Summertime, oh summertime.

What a romantic night it was. Despite the sadness I felt and the frustrated desire to be desired, the beauty of the scene had an effect. I wanted to memorize it, to hold the details for a future version of myself who would, I imagined, look back on this moment with heartache. I pitied that future self, filled with regret for the passage of time. Or maybe what I felt was more complicated than pity. Maybe it was the fear that she wouldn't feel nostalgia or regret, wouldn't even remember the importance of this version of me. That I would be outgrown, left behind, not by my mother but by myself.

Monica heaved a deep sigh and rested her head on my shoulder. I leaned my cheek against her hair and closed my eyes, listening to the back and forth motion of the waves, the music of the moon. To the wanting that would not end.

LIKE LOVE

The train chuffed, engine humming, metal wheels ready to slide along metal tracks. I had already pulled the window down and reached through the open space, stretching my arm toward Tomas, who couldn't quite close the distance between us. Then the train lurched forward. "I miss you!" he called, tears suddenly leaking from his blue eyes, and the world began to spin.

This is not a love story.

When we travel, Cynthia Ozick writes in "The Shock of Teapots," the powers of observation we had in childhood return to us. Unmoored from everyday life, we pay keen attention. "[N]othing is not for notice, nothing is banal, nothing is ordinary: not a rock, not the shoulder of a passer-by, not a teapot." And not Tomas, who had walked toward me across the courtyard of the youth hostel in Hamburg, Germany, beginning to talk even before he reached me, as if we were already friends.

"There is not space here," he frowned. The accent was German, as was his look: jeans and a crisp white tee shirt, the sleeves of a gray sweater tied around his throat. He was tall, broad, with wide eyes and a natural wave to his sandy brown hair. His casual way of speaking made me wonder if I seemed familiar to him, too. Maybe our paths had crossed on the ferry from Dover to Calais the previous afternoon, or maybe he had been on the overnight train that arrived in the city center an hour ago.

I checked my watch: 8:02 a.m. "How can it be full already?"

Tomas swatted the air with his hand. "They accept only people which have some special card. Otherwise, no bed."

On a different day, I might have nodded in sympathy and gone inside. But just a few minutes before, on the last leg of my walk from the train station, when I arrived at a fork in the road that didn't appear on my map, a middle-aged man wearing only pajama pants began shouting from a fourth-floor balcony. Bracing for a cat-call, I shielded my eyes with one hand and shouted back, "Ich spreche nicht Deutsch!" The man pressed his palms together and tilted his head against them, pantomiming sleep. Only then did I understand the word he'd been shouting, *jugendherberge.* I called back, "Ja!" eager to find the youth hostel, and he pointed to the street ahead, then gestured left, right, and up a big, winding hill, at the top of which, owing to the good luck travel summons, stood Tomas.

"Here," I said, digging into the side pocket of my backpack for an international hostel card. "My boyfriend and I got this together, but he's not here yet. This should get us both in." I handed the card to Tomas, who scrutinized the photograph with a scowl.

"He is not me, clearly."

"So what?" I responded with my American understanding of bendable rules. "The card is for two people, and we are two people. I'm sure they won't mind."

Tomas was skeptical, but the clerk didn't even glance at him while checking us in. He just collected our money, handed over locker keys, and directed us to the men's and women's dormitories. Tomas thanked me profusely and I shrugged, having done so little to help, and went to store my backpack. Then, feeling light and unburdened and eager to explore, I headed back to the main entrance, where Tomas was waiting. "Please," he said, smiling broadly and placing an open palm on my shoulder. "I will thank you with some coffee."

In just five days of traveling, I'd been surprised by the response to a young woman alone. Several men on the street in London had commented on my backpack and my courage in tones that said courage meant foolishness. In one Tube station, an Algerian man clucked his teeth—even though I wasn't wearing the backpack at the time—and insisted he would accompany me wherever I was going. On a bench beside the Thames, three Italian men said, "Sola? No, no!" and tried to convince me to follow them. And even on the Channel ferry, a young German woman offered tips about the best places to meet men in Hamburg, as if there could be no other goal for me there. But I wasn't looking for romance on this month-long journey. Or rather, I wasn't looking for the kind of romance that involves another person. As Pico Iyer writes, "we travel, in essence, to become young fools again—to slow time down and get taken in, and fall in love once more." There's no "with" to the "falling in love," there's just the glorious feeling of surprise and surrender that travel brings.

It felt good not to be alone in Hamburg. After Tomas unfolded his map and plotted a route, I relaxed for the first time since getting on the plane in New York five days before. I absorbed the familiar foreignness, staring at petite cars, at weathered brick buildings with ornate parapets, at street signs with cryptic words like "Fahrradstraße" (bicycle street) or bright images like a blue circle rimmed in red with a diagonal red line across it (no parking). Now and then I paused to photograph the stone lintel of a doorway or a narrow brick street lined with colorful buildings, but Tomas was in charge; I simply walked and reacted.

Soon we came upon a Bavarian bakery whose name caught Tomas's attention. With its low ceilings and dark woodwork, the bakery could have leapt from the pages of my college German textbook, the one I'd studied for a year without learning enough. We sat upstairs, in a room that was hardly above normal first-floor height, beside a window with a perfect view of the street. I watched people going about their Saturday morning routines, and a sense of accomplishment washed over me. This was exactly what I'd imagined when I planned a trip to Europe.

Tomas and I traded stories. He came from a village in the south, outside Freiburg, and had never traveled this far north before. He'd just graduated from college, and before starting business school in the fall, he decided to take a few days off work and explore. "My girlfriend doesn't come, which leaves me here alone," he explained, an earnest expression on his face. I asked why he chose Hamburg, and he listed several museums and the musical *Cats*, which he was eager to see.

I explained that I was a year out of college and working in a restaurant, with no idea what to do next, and that I'd taken this trip in the hopes of being inspired in some direction. I was traveling alone for the first two weeks before meeting my boyfriend in Munich, and I'd just come from London, which was nice but didn't fit my mood. I wanted to visit small cities, places I could cover mostly on foot, getting a sense of what everyday life is like. Because I was due to visit a friend in Copenhagen on Monday, I had gone to Victoria Station on Friday and asked a ticket seller where I might spend the weekend. He said his wife had once visited Hamburg and had quite a good time, and a train was leaving in an hour. "So here I am," I said, shrugging, while Tomas stared as if I'd grown a new appendage.

He'd spent weeks planning his four-day trip and had arrived with a detailed itinerary. "I cannot imagine doing something like you," he said before breaking into a wide smile. "But you see, we are perfect! I have not a hostel card, and you helped me. But you have not a plan for seeing Hamburg, and I will guide!"

I tried to read the expression on his face. Did Tomas feel obligated to take care of me? Sorry for a woman traveling alone? Attracted? His expression was wide and open, eyebrows arcing in a way that seemed merely friendly. I could tell he was a person who liked things to proceed logically, and since I shared that trait, I said I'd be happy to spend the afternoon sightseeing with him. We toasted the arrangement with coffee cups, the ceramic clink accompanied by the blare of trumpets. Outside the window, a marching band was turning the corner and heading down our block. "Hamburg welcomes us," Tomas grinned, raising his cup again.

Travel has a way of compressing time and, alternately, expanding it. Weeks go by quickly, but days often stretch, accommodating more than we thought possible. Tomas and I walked through a maze of streets in the old city, crossed a bridge to the enormous plaza in front of the Rathaus, the nineteenth-century town hall whose carved stone and green copper roof gave me chills because I really was here, on a bold, European adventure. After that we followed a path along Inner Alster Lake, bought lunchtime sausages from a street vendor, and despite the clouds that rolled in with occasional raindrops, sat on a bench to eat them. All the while we talked and talked, until by mid-afternoon, we had moved through the initial stages of friendship into something strangely intimate. We told stories, chided each other's taste in music, became bossy.

"You won't like that flavor. Try this instead."

"If you're cold, put your sweater on."

"You must buy this as a souvenir."

Tomas led us to the Heinrich-Hertz-Turm, a radio communications tower that was the tallest building in Hamburg and, from my perspective, an eyesore. Its space-age look, a needle wrapped with circular observation floors and satellite dishes, was the opposite of the historic sites I craved, but Tomas insisted, "We must see the view. Come!" So I went.

Even with the clouds, the observation floor allowed us to see in every direction. We traced the Elbe River to the port below the youth hostel, located the Rathaus and the spires of several churches we'd passed. We leaned together, map open, pointing from page to reality, then separated, each of us captivated by some aspect of the view. Several times Tomas sidled up to me and began speaking in German, and when I replied, "Ich verstehe nicht," his face reddened. "I cannot believe it! You seem so much like me that I don't remember you're American."

How often do we say that? You seem so much like me. Even in our regular lives, at home where we speak the language and understand the customs, how often do we feel such affinity with another person?

My first serious romantic relationship had entered its fourth year. My boyfriend was an engineer by day and a daredevil on weekends, racing motorcycles, skiing off-trail, helping out friends who owned a fireworks company by hand-rolling bombs and then blowing them up in shows. He was also a hunter and fisherman, prone to going off to the woods, alone. When we started dating I assumed it would be a casual, short affair, but some combination of thrill and inertia made me adapt to his priorities and accept that, while I was more important to him than most other people, opportunities for fun ranked above everything else in his life.

Because of that, I didn't expect him to object to my month-long backpacking adventure, and I certainly didn't expect him to argue that it was dangerous. This was a man who viewed blizzard warnings as a reason to jump in the car and head for the nearest slopes, a man who had taught me to shoot rifles and handguns and who sometimes piloted a motorboat on the Hudson River while I water-skied behind and, when the engine started to sputter, took a screwdriver to it with no one at the helm. So I was stunned when he urged me to reconsider and even more stunned when, after I'd booked my flights and designed a Euro-pass itinerary, he insisted on meeting me at the halfway point.

I'd been ambivalent about this plan, but London was such a lonely experience that I began to look forward to the second half of the trip. Now in Hamburg, the real benefit to traveling alone became clear: If my boyfriend had been with me, Tomas and I may not have met and certainly wouldn't have become friends, and I would have missed the opportunity to tour the city with someone who was making my first visit to a non-English-speaking country both comfortable and fun. I wondered what other experiences might close off once my boyfriend arrived.

I also wondered what to make of this connection with Tomas. It was perplexing to have met a complete stranger with whom I got along so easily, so effortlessly. How was that possible? The most readily available way to understand this new encounter was through romance, and specifically through the serendipitous story of finding a soul mate while traveling. Was Tomas, I wondered, someone with whom I could fall in love? Or barring that, someone with whom I might have a short, discrete affair?

That possibility floated through the day as I watched for signs of desire in myself and in him. In the evening we returned to the hostel for jackets, then walked the grounds overlooking the port on the Elbe. We took pictures of each other beside an enormous patch of blue hydrangeas, against a background of light-gray skies and dark-gray tankers, and the combination of beauty and grit made us sit down on a boulder to admire it. I snuck glances at Tomas, trying to imagine kissing him, nestling into his chest, holding his hand as we walked around town. With his thick, wavy hair, wide cheeks, and bright blue eyes, he was certainly attractive. But was I attracted?

Tomas's shoulder nudged my own. "Look at this bird," he said, pointing into the air. I leaned toward him and squinted, inhaling his scent, which was earthy and sweet and homey. My eyes closed, and I let go for a moment of the thinking process and paid attention to associations. Tomas smelled like a kitchen, a basement, a back garden, like family dinners that morph into arguments, like a present moment tethered to the past. He smelled like a cousin, someone you've always known, someone fun and dependable but not someone whose skin you want to feel against yours. I opened my eyes, watched the large, heron-like bird glide onto a stone wall beside the water and then watched Tomas watching it, bent forward with elbows on his knees. I'd never cheated on my boyfriend, although I wasn't sure the same could be said of him, and if I wanted to do so now, he'd never find out. The idea of a secret affair, a little gift to myself on this solo journey was appealing, and I made space in my mind for desire to make itself known. But for whatever reason, hormones or pheromones or the opposite of "opposites attract," it wasn't there.

Nor were there any hints of desire on Tomas's part. When he tired of watching the bird, he stood and said, in a matter-of-fact tone without subtext, "I have hunger. Do you?"

We wound back toward the historic Altstadt, where a Turkish street festival welcomed us with music and the smell of barbeque. We lingered, ordering spicy eggplant and rice accompanied by wheat beer, which we enjoyed standing beside one of many tall tables set up in the street. A band of five men played instruments that looked like the cousins of clarinets and lutes, and we clapped along, mesmerized, for their entire set. "What luck!" Tomas kept saying. It was a perfect day, so many events seemingly arranged just for our benefit, with no price to them. I felt full and happy and, by 9 p.m., almost too tired to go on. Having slept fitfully in a train compartment the night before, I began to crave the narrow bed of the hostel.

When Tomas realized this, he pulled out the map and quickly plotted the most direct route back. But along the way we passed a biergarten, an enormous, raucous hall with pots of geraniums spilling from the wide entrance and music cascading into the street. "Have you been to one of these?" Tomas asked, and the excitement on his face gave me a second wind.

Rows of long wooden tables filled the hall, each of them so crowded that we had to squeeze onto benches at the end of a table and flag down a woman dressed like the St. Pauli girl to order. Accordion music projected throughout the hall, forcing everyone to shout. Tomas and I looked around, absorbing the good cheer. Most everyone had come with a group, or maybe they'd been assimilated into groups, and lively toasts were continuously made. Our wheat beer arrived in plastic steins so big I admitted defeat before the first sip. "I could never drink this much in one sitting," I shouted, and Tomas shook his head. "Me, too!"

We leaned close across the table as Tomas described the biergarten in his village, smaller than this but even more festive. Then he added, "We must do one thing that is very traditional, yes? For luck." He explained how we would hold our steins, entwine our arms, sip our beer, and then, before our arms untangled themselves, lean forward and kiss on the lips. "What?" I shouted. Tomas laughed, his cheeks coloring, and pointed to the young people toward the middle of our table whose arms quickly intertwined and let go after they kissed one another.

Tomas and I followed suit. After our kiss, which was brief and chaste, we held each other's gaze for a moment, smiling slightly, eyebrows raised. Negotiating. We could kiss again, and kiss again after that, falling down the beer-induced rabbit hole that would make this day more recognizable. I had the sense that if one of us made a move, the other would follow along, that we had only to lean a little closer to accept our roles in a ready-made storyline. But what sort of experience did we want? How much of a mark should this weekend make? Even a secret affair would go home with each of us, and maybe we

wanted it to, maybe we both craved a way to begin exit-
ing the relationships we'd temporarily left. Or maybe not.
It was the end of a long day. We were tired. And most
importantly, we were too much alike to let circumstanc-
es override our inclinations. One of us blinked, the other
looked away, and that was that.

To awaken on a Sunday morning in the stale-cracker
cloud of bodies at rest, many bodies and many beds, with
not much space between them, is oddly comforting. I lifted my head and saw that every bed was full, although
bright sun seeped around the window shades. I had no
idea what time it was and thought for a long while about
how to approach the day.

Tomas and I had said good night in the lobby without making further plans. I didn't want him to feel obligated to guide me around again today, but I also didn't
want to blow him off after he'd been so kind yesterday.
I decided to shower, dress, and leave a note for him at
the front desk, telling him I'd gone out for breakfast and
might see him later. But at my locker in the hall, a folded
piece of notebook paper stuck out from the lock. "Guten
morgen!" it read. "Want to visit a model train museum? I
wait downstairs."

And so it went. Breakfast, a long walk, sightseeing,
lunch. Now, on the second day, we had a history, a common past. We whispered jokes, ate off each other's plates,
got annoyed and let it show. At the model train museum,
I read aloud from an English placard. "Built in 1902 . . ."
and Tomas interrupted. "Why must Americans say nine-
teen-OH-two instead of nineteen-hundred and two? Is
this laziness?"

His sarcastic tone was even more pointed than his words, so I snapped back, "Why don't you keep your German superiority to yourself for once?"

He glared and I turned my back, heading into another room. It was unlike me to be so snotty. When my boyfriend and I argued, we both grew quiet and waited for the anger to pass. Now I discovered the pleasure in blowing off steam. It felt good to say something rude and not rush to apologize, to let my temper flare into an implicit threat: I'll walk away from you and not look back.

A few minutes later, an elbow nudged my side. "This place is bored," Tomas said. "Want to eat ice cream?"

I said yes, and we made our way back to the street.

On that second day in Hamburg, as the surroundings began to seem familiar and the language to divide itself into separate words, some of which I understood, my energy plummeted. After lunch, which consisted of another sausage eaten on a park bench, I confessed to Tomas that I couldn't keep walking. "Anyplace else we go has to be by bus or train," I said, massaging my calf muscles.

"But you see, it's perfect!" Tomas said, sitting up straight and opening the map. He always had an idea, and it was always a good one.

Soon we were on the S-Bahn riding into the suburbs. Tomas was curious about what it might be like to live in Hamburg, and we scrutinized the neighborhoods that passed, pointing out houses we liked and discussing their brick construction. "Do you live in a wooden house?" he asked, and I said I did. "But wood burns," he stated, an expression of alarm on his face. "Everything inside a brick house also burns," I countered. That prompted a discussion of the Great Fire of London and the Chicago

Fire and the firebombing of Hamburg at the end of World War II. We scrolled through past history lessons, digging up clumps of fact and pressing them into a mosaic of trans-Atlantic education. I'd always been embarrassed by how much I didn't know about geography and history, but chatting with Tomas felt like stretching muscles, taking stock, finding common ground. Instead of feeling with shame that I ought to know more, I felt curious, excited to learn.

We rode nearly to the end of the line, then got off the train and waited for the return trip. On the small platform, nestled in a quiet neighborhood of single-story homes, we pulled our sweaters close and shook our heads at the clouds that had arrived yet again. "It is warmer in the south," Tomas remarked, and I said I looked forward to going there. He asked what time my train to Copenhagen left in the morning. "Early," I said. "8:15."

Then, silence. The S-Bahn arrived and we sat down, gazing toward the opposite side of the tracks we'd just traveled. We rode back through the same neighborhoods, not commenting on the houses or the parks, no longer imagining what it would be like to live here or talking about the future. The contrast with just a little while ago was stark: then we'd been animated, excited, on an adventure, and now we were coming back, coming down, entering the last stage of this curious weekend.

Back in Hamburg, we ate slices of pizza for dinner and walked to the Reeperbahn, the red-list district where the theater hosting *Cats* was located. Tomas bought a ticket for the following evening's show, and his full-body excitement at realizing this dream made me wish I could go, too. He suggested I stay one more day, but that was impossible, since the friend I planned to visit in Copenhagen would be leaving on a business trip in a few days. And anyway, I didn't want to spend more time in Hamburg. I liked the city a great deal, but I was ready to unmoor myself again, enter unfamiliar territory, experience the frisson of anxiety and expectation a new place brings. That's what this trip was about, jarring myself into some new perspective that might help me navigate the future at home. Still, the sadness of endings was upon us, and despite not wanting to stay, I didn't entirely want to go.

As we walked past plate-glass windows decorated with whips and leather vests, past signs announcing "Sexy Shop" and "Bar Erotik," silence overtook us. This was a different Hamburg than the one we'd been exploring; here, the undercurrents of intimacy were on the surface, advertised in neon. I wasn't sure how to respond or whether to respond, but soon Tomas waved his hand back and forth, gesturing toward the entire block. "This is life," he said, shrugging, and I shrugged back, and then the awkwardness was gone and we were ourselves again, only more so. Waiting to cross a street, I felt Tomas's hand against my back as he leaned in to say something, and the only surprise was how natural this felt, how impossible that forty-eight hours before I hadn't known him.

It was close to 10 p.m. when we approached the hostel, climbing slowly up the zigzag path to the courtyard where we'd met. Tomas shook his head and laughed. "I can't believe it. Hardly do I know you, yet I will miss you very much."

"I'll miss you, too. But at least you have *Cats* to look forward to."

"And my bicycle."

"What bicycle?" I asked.

Tomas pointed to the full bike rack in front of the hostel and explained that he'd brought his bike on the train from Freiberg but hadn't ridden it yet.

I fell all over myself apologizing—how much more Tomas could have seen of Hamburg by bike, how lovely that would have been, how sorry I was to have taken up all his time—until we reached the door and he hugged me tight. Again I felt the romance narrative circling us, looking for a way to take hold. But it wasn't a romantic hug. It was a hug filled with friendly appreciation.

"See me in the morning," Tomas said, and I promised I would.

It is easier to leave than to be left. The traveler has unfamiliarity to look forward to, new sites and schedules, the challenge of negotiating difference. Tomas and I were both travelers in Hamburg, but the place was familiar now, less exciting than it had been two days ago. Early on Monday morning, as he carried my backpack to the train station, Tomas seemed sadder than I felt. A journey lay ahead for me, and at the other end a new city and an old friend. But for Tomas this last full day in Hamburg marked the end of his too-short adventure.

On the platform we hugged goodbye and kissed each other on both cheeks. We had already exchanged addresses, which might mean a postcard or two at most. "Enjoy *Cats*," I said, and Tomas smiled. "Enjoy the rest of your life."

I nodded, eyes filling with inexplicable tears, and got on the train.

The car was designed with a corridor on the right and compartments on the left, each with a sliding door and, inside, three seats facing three seats. I found my assigned space beside the window and hoisted my backpack onto the luggage rack, chest heaving and sorrowful sounds threatening to escape from my throat. "Get it together," I thought. I've always been sentimental, prone to crying at the ends of books and movies, but this depth of emotion was out of proportion to the experience.

I sat down, trying not to look at the other passengers, a gentleman directly across from me and a woman wearing a business suit near the door, and glanced out the window where Tomas, just on the other side of the glass, was jumping and waving. I laughed and examined the window frame, discovering a metal bar that, when pressed, allowed the pane to slide down.

"What are you doing?" I shouted, and he laughed. "Hello! Bon voyage!"

"Danke!"

We exchanged a few words about the day and the evening ahead, repeating phrases we'd already said, and then the train whistle sounded, followed by the whoosh of hydraulic brakes.

"Auf wiedersehen!" Tomas called, his face reddening and tears springing to his eyes. He reached up, motioning for me to grasp his hand, and I stuck my arm out the window to the shoulder, but we were too far apart to connect, so I retracted my arm and waved again. The train began to move. I pulled back into the car, wanting to sit down and take deep breaths until the choking sensation disappeared, but Tomas called out, "I miss you!" and began to run. All the way down the platform, until I thought he might dive out of the station into the sunlight of the open tracks, Tomas kept pace with the train, waving and calling goodbye, tears streaming down his wide, handsome face.

Why? I wondered, wiping my eyes and blowing my nose, kilometer after kilometer. Now I cried openly, aware that the other passengers in the compartment would assume I was heartbroken. What a scene. All weekend

Tomas and I had dodged the overdone romance story, and at the last minute it had caught up to us anyway. But instead of feeling embarrassed by our cliché, I felt fortified, blessed, elated even as I wept. What an unexpected, sweet, marvelous thing to be part of. So what if we'd spent only forty-eight hours together? So what if we weren't attracted to each other in a physical way and I hadn't particularly wanted to stay longer with him? This had been the most romantic weekend of my life.

The man across from me turned out to be a college professor who spoke English. He asked about my trip, and I had the sense that he was trying to distract me from heartache. I wanted to explain that I wasn't sad, that I hardly knew the guy, but what would that have meant? Instead, I asked him to recommend a small city, even smaller than Hamburg, that I might visit after Copenhagen, on my way to Munich. His face lit up, and we spread my map across our knees, heads bent together as he described sites and summer festivals, circling locations in black ink.

Soon I did feel better. And something else besides: the goodbye Tomas and I shared took on the shape and texture of real emotion. I understood, not for the first time and not for the last, but during a period of life when the lesson seemed particularly important, that sometimes the vast possibility signaled by romance is all there is. And that doesn't diminish its power. What Tomas and I each felt was not love, but it was so much like love that all the way to Copenhagen, and for a long time after—decades, in fact—the air seemed to crackle with its spell.

EVENINGS AT THE
COLLEGEVIEW DINER

If you sat on one of the bright red stools and swiveled so
your back leaned against the counter, if you looked out
the diner's front windows, across the small parking lot
and the busy street, between the roofs of the tract houses and past distant trees on a hill, you could almost see
the main building of the local community college. But
not quite. That's how everything was at the Collegeview
Diner: not quite.

And yet I'd been happy when the owner called me one
March afternoon for an interview. I was sixteen years old
and lacked transportation to any of the starter jobs my
friends held at fast food restaurants and grocery stores.
The diner was just around the corner from our house and
familiar because my father and I had been going there
every few weeks since it opened the year before. We were
tired of our own kitchen and the various meals we baked
or broiled—fish sticks, steak, pork chops, frozen French
fries—everything doused in the only spice we knew: gar-
lic salt.

I had good associations with the diner, which always smelled clean and cool, like the inside of a freezer. My father and I would sit at the counter, facing a mirrored pie case, and order hamburgers or grilled cheese, coffee for him and Tab soda for me. Shirley, the owner's wife, a middle-aged waitress whose left hand waved and flourished as if to music, described the business to us, how it was slow in the evening but packed for breakfast and lunch. "The place just needs some time," she said, prompting my father to suggest I leave our phone number, in case they needed to hire another waitress at some point.

At the interview, Louie came out of the kitchen in a white apron streaked with what looked like ketchup, his bushy black hair and green eyes seeming to accuse me. "I didn't call you," he said in a Greek accent so thick it took a moment for me to decipher his words. "Look." He opened the register, lifted the change drawer, and removed a slip of paper. "This is who I called." He turned the page toward me, showing the blocky letters and numbers.

"Yes," I smiled. "That's me."

Louie stared for a moment before lifting his hands and grasping the sides of his head. "No, no, not *you*." He watched the ceiling for a long time, then scowled at me and admitted he had no one for the Saturday shift, 6 a.m. to 4 p.m. I said I'd be there, bright and early.

Ah, the American diner, a place of welcome and respite. Its roots stretch back to the food wagons of the late nineteenth century, to Providence, Rhode Island, where an industrious seventeen-year-old sold coffee and sandwiches to late-night crowds. The idea was so lucrative it spread through major cities, and in the early twentieth century, the Worcester Lunch Car Company in Massachusetts began manufacturing stationary diners. Over the next decades, the diner morphed again and again, first into the "modernized" stainless steel structure we now romanticize and then into storefront cafes like the one in Edward Hopper's painting *Nighthawks*. The common denominator was inexpensive food and bottomless cups of coffee, and eventually, on the east coast, the diner more often than not was Greek, with long menus on which gyros and spanakopita crowded against hot cakes and rice pudding.

From the outside, the Collegeview Diner looked like a quaint café, with cedar shake siding and multi-paned windows, but inside, it was a diner: Formica tables with bright red chairs, a matching L-shaped counter with swivel stools. Behind the counters, stainless steel shelving hung from the walls and an ice cream cooler stored drums of vanilla, chocolate, and strawberry, beside a toppings station with sauces, whipped cream, and cherries. As a fiercely pretty young waitress showed me around in preparation for Saturday's shift, I listened intently—takeout coffee cups are here, dirty dishes go there, be sure to restock everything for the Monday morning rush—and knew my first day would be a nightmare.

It was. I had so little experience to draw on that my first shift unfolded like a Carol Burnett comedy routine in which a bumbling young woman has no common sense. Wearing stiff black pants and a white blouse, an apron borrowed from Shirley tied tight around my waist, I served my first customer half a cup of coffee on an overflowing saucer, then made two more trips for a creamer and a spoon.

The depth of my naivete showed after I took the man's order and ducked into the kitchen, where Louie's sleepy face appeared above the shelf between me and the grill. I was supposed to shout the order, but it was so early I couldn't bear to raise my voice, so I walked around the steam table and met Louie on his territory.

"OK," I said. "This man wants eggs."

"He wants *what*?"

"Eggs. That's what he told me."

"Here," Louie said, opening the small refrigerator to the side of the grill. He took out two eggs and motioned as if to hand them to me.

"What are you doing?" I asked, not taking them.

"You say he wants eggs, here's eggs."

It took me a second to decode the accent, and then I laughed. "He wants them cooked."

"Oh, I see. He wants *cooked* eggs. OK, then. How the fuck am I supposed to cook them?"

"On the grill?"

Louie's hairline flinched. "No, dummy, how am I supposed to cook them? Scrambled? Over easy? Looking at the ceiling?"

"Oh!" I said, relieved. If I could understand the problem, solving it seemed within reach.

When I asked the customer how he wanted his eggs cooked, he rolled his eyes and shook his head, which I took as irritation with my inexperience. In fact, he was irritated with Louie, who knew exactly how the man wanted his eggs—sunny side up, no potatoes, rye toast—because that's what he ate for breakfast every morning, six days a week, sitting on the same stool, reading the *New York Daily News*. But on my first day of work, everything seemed to be my fault.

By 8:00 a.m., the diner had transformed into something I couldn't believe existed in the neighborhood: a hot spot. Customers sat along the entire counter and at most of the tables, waiting for coffee, eggs (cooked how?), toast (white, wheat, or rye?), juice (apple or orange?), pancakes and french toast (with bacon? sausage? ham?), breakfast sandwiches (on toast? hard roll? English muffin?), or they waited for their checks, or for their change at the register, or for take-out coffee orders—light, light and sweet, black with sugar, dark without. For several hours, until things settled down after lunch, Louie cooked the food and waited on half the customers, while I worked twice as hard as he did to keep up with the other half.

Through all the chaos, Louie's voice offered steady sarcasm and outright insults. "What's wrong with you? Are you a moron? Is your brain damaged?" He spoke loudly, in front of customers who seemed as embarrassed as I was. Several times I thought about untying my apron and heading for the door, but as mortifying as it was to suck at my first job, the prospect of losing it seemed worse.

During the lunch rush, which was less harried than breakfast, Louie stayed mostly in the kitchen, and when it was over, he rang the bell and shoved a plate of grilled cheese and French fries toward me. "Eat this," he said, and I did, taking bites between clearing tables, totaling bills, and working the register. The food got me through until the diner emptied out around 3:30. When I finally sat down, my legs felt like concrete, and with only half an hour until closing, my thoughts turned to the inevitable: being fired. Fine, I thought, fantasizing about walking home, going to my room, stripping off my clothes, and crawling into bed. It was possible I'd sleep straight through until the next morning, when everything about this day would seem like a bad dream, and then I'd never set foot in the diner again.

Louie told me to cash in my tips so he'd have change in the register for Monday. I retrieved the cup I'd stashed under the counter and spilled its contents out, then stacked the coins into piles. I counted them twice, shocked that they added up to forty-nine dollars. Plus ten one-dollar bills and the hourly pay Louie owed me, and I'd made almost eighty dollars on my first day at work. Eighty dollars! In a single day! My friends had to work twice as many hours to clear that much.

"I don't get it," Louie grumbled as he paid me in cash. "This was a slow day. And you're the worst waitress I've ever seen. Understand? The worst!"

I didn't care what he said at that point. I had money in my pocket, all my own. I laughed out loud, and Louie shook his head back and forth, eventually cracking a smile.

When I started to work, my father and I had been on our own for three years. Before that we'd lived with my mother as a buffer between us. She was the parent who hugged my brother and me, who asked what we needed to eat, to drink, to make us happy. She signed our permission slips and talked about how school had gone each day. She was the last person we saw before bed and the first to say good morning when we woke.

Because my father worked second shift, he'd always been asleep when my brother and I left for school in the morning and didn't get home until long after we were in bed at night. On weekends, he spent most of his time working on our house, tearing out walls, installing new windows and doors, replacing broken shingles, painting. He was proud of this work, especially once strangers began stopping their cars in front of our house and waving him over to say how terrific the place looked. My father was making something of himself, something for his family, and the evidence was there on our busy street for all the world to see.

But the improvement in the house corresponded with a deterioration in our home. Just as the renovation finished and there was going to be time and money for other things, my mother left, taking Michael and me with her.

During the months after we moved in with Jan, the term "family" seemed like a broad concept that could be molded to any situation. I tried to think of her two boys as my brothers and her girl as my sister, and I tried to be happy for my mother, who giggled and flirted and made out with this new partner in front of us, the way she'd never done with my father. But over time I grew disillusioned. The voice Jan often used when speaking to my mother, which sounded like she was talking to a pet, began to grate on me, and soon they quarreled about money and time and how to discipline a brood of disgruntled kids.

Then one day after school my mother met me at the bus stop. "Pack your things," she said cheerfully. "We're going home." I didn't understand. "This is just too hard," she said, taking a long drag on a cigarette. "Come on, don't you want your own bedroom again?"

Of course I did. But as imperfect as life in the country was, with seven people sharing a bathroom and chaos at every mealtime, it was more peaceful than life with my father. I didn't want to go back to the fighting, the fear, the sense that my parents were headed toward something irrevocable. So I told my mother it was a bad idea.

"Too late," she chirped, "the movers come tomorrow."

During the eight-month reconciliation period that followed, there was no fighting, no waking in the middle of the night with my heart racing. My father cleaned and did laundry and spoke in a voice so gentle I hardly recognized it. But my mother was in terrible shape. She chain-smoked and lost weight and talked to Jan on the phone for hours every day until it became clear that she would leave again, and that I would have to face the vow I made before we returned: "If we go back," I'd told her, "I'm not moving again." I meant that I was done bouncing around, that I wanted her to make a decision and stick by it. But I also meant that I might not always choose her, that if she wasn't careful, she could lose me. It didn't occur to me then that the opposite might also be true: if I wasn't careful, I could lose her.

When my mother left my father the second time, she and I broke up. That's how it felt, like a rupture, a turning away, like the love of my life was gone.

The reason was partly logistical. According to the separation agreement, my mother was not allowed into my father's house, so if she wanted to see me, she had to pick me up and take me to her place. But I didn't want to sit in her living room crammed with Jan's furniture plus the tables and recliner my mother had insisted on taking from our house. I didn't want to feel like a guest in the home where Jan's kids lounged around, where her sons bickered with my brother, where my brother barely spoke to me. When Michael stayed at our house on weekends, we got along fine, but in the place where he lived, we were strangers.

For three years, my mother called now and then to invite me over, even though I almost always had other plans: I was spending the night at a friend's, had a test to study for, was going to the movies. Every few months I'd accept her invitation, and after dinner my mother would wash the dishes and I'd dry, snooping through cupboards as I put things away. My mother's kitchen was a land of plenty, the shelves stocked with tomato paste and kidney beans, large sacks of flour, boxes of raisins. Ingredients piled against one other, ready at a moment's notice to combine into a fragrant steam. I'd lean into the cupboards and sniff, inhaling *home,* and then once the dishes were done, my mother drove me back to my father's house, a place of ordered, echoing space. After each of these visits, I felt so sad I couldn't go back for a while.

Then I started to work at the diner, a public place where my mother had every right to be. She could visit without calling first or asking my permission. And she could leave a tip behind on the counter, for which she knew I would have to feel grateful.

Hopper's *Nighthawks* depicts diner life in the 1940s, the people dressed smartly, the only woman accompanied by a man. The first time I saw the painting in the Art Institute of Chicago, I gasped aloud, so familiar was the mood. Plate glass windows frame a triangular counter, with a lone man sitting on one side and a couple on the other. Between them, a cook in a white shirt and paper hat bends over, talking to the couple as, I imagine, he rinses something in a sink, and although everyone's posture conveys a bit of fatigue—it's nighttime after all, as the darkness beyond the windows shows—there's nothing particularly sad in the scene. And yet the mood, the browns and greens and yellow, the light and the loneliness held at bay, call to mind the kind of mournful resignation that allows us to get through heartache.

Although I had made my mother promise not to come in on my first day of work, I encouraged her to stop by that second Saturday. I thought things would be easier then and wanted her to see that I was working hard, making my own money, handling my own life.

Not until she walked through the door, eyes scanning the crowded room, did I see my mistake. I hadn't believed Louie the previous week when he said business was slow. Now, everywhere I looked, people craned their necks hoping to order or stood beside the register shifting from foot to foot, money in hand, and every thirty seconds Louie rang the bell to signal another order up.

When my mother came in, I motioned to the only empty stool at the counter. I brought her a cup of coffee with a spoon and a creamer, not a drop spilled onto the saucer. Then I paused for a moment and looked at her. Short, permanent-waved brown hair, pale blue eyes, pink lipstick. With her sitting and me standing, in a position to bring whatever she wanted, I felt a burst of happy surprise. Here was my mother, a guest in my life apart from her.

"Hey!" Louie called from the kitchen, bell ringing wildly. "Take these pancakes!"

My mother ordered two eggs over easy and announced to the man beside her that one person could never handle all this. "It's ridiculous," she said, laughing nervously. Midway through breakfast her language strengthened. "This is bullshit! How can he make you work all alone?" She offered to clear tables and refill coffee cups, but I said no way. Absolutely no way. If what Louie said was true, that one girl always handled the Saturday crowd, I would become that girl. I'd make myself faster and more efficient. The next time my mother came in, she'd marvel.

Later in the morning, after my mother had gone and the rush had subsided, leaving dirty dishes on every table and along the counter, my father appeared. He sat in our usual spot in front of the pie case and said, "My God almighty, I don't know how you can do this."

"Me neither," I replied, piling plates and cups into a bus pan. Seeing him from this side of the counter, the way Shirley had on our Friday night visits, made me dizzy. He looked like the other middle-aged men hunched over cups of coffee, packs of cigarettes in their shirt pockets, disappointment settled on their shoulders.

"I'll take an egg omelet," he said, and my face flushed because what other kind of omelet was there? He meant a *plain* omelet, and the fact that I knew this, that I understood, on my second day of work, something about the world that my father didn't, stung my eyes.

Louie came out of the kitchen and nodded to my father, smiling. "At least she's bringing some business."

After that, Louie kept his comments to himself for a while, and I began to catch a rhythm. When a new table sat down, I brought them coffee just in case, and if one person declined, I dropped that cup in front of someone at the counter. I brought dirty dishes with me each time I headed to the kitchen and asked every single person who ordered eggs how they wanted them cooked. Louie seemed to notice my improvement, but as the day wore on, he turned nasty again. When I couldn't find clean towels in the storeroom, he called me blind; when I made a mistake on someone's check, he called me stupid. I counted the minutes until I'd be released from his abuse while also marveling at how my tips had overflowed into a second cup.

At 3:00 p.m., just an hour before closing, there were only a handful of people in the diner, two women at a table and a few guys scattered along the counters. Everyone was eating or had paid, and my legs throbbed in the slow pace of the homestretch. I cleared a dirty table, stacking plates, cups, and saucers neatly inside one another, and carried the stack into the kitchen. Then, moving awkwardly to set everything on the sink, I lost control of two cups, which tumbled to the floor, ceramic shattering. The room brightened and spun. Pricks of exhaustion shot through my central nervous system. As I bent to pick up the pieces, Louie appeared beside me with a broom, and for once he didn't yell, he just looked down at me and said, in a voice dripping with disgust, "That's beautiful. Just beautiful."

For a long time I'd been pretending everything was fine. When girls at school talked about going shopping with their moms, I nodded brightly, as if I, too, had that experience. When Monica's mother started calling me her second daughter, I feigned appreciation, even though the difference between a real mother and a borrowed one is stark. Sometimes I fantasized about my mother dying, which would at least have the benefit of allowing people to understand the pain I carried. Instead my mother, who I loved and resented and missed so deeply I often woke in the middle of the night in tears, had left me behind and never talked about it. I carried my anger, cradling it tightly, afraid to release it in a powerful burst, because once it was gone, what would I have? I didn't know then about anger's endless capacity for regeneration. I only knew that Louie's words were like a magic password, releasing it.

In one quick motion, I bent over, grabbed what was left of a cup, and hurled it against the sink, shouting loud enough for the customers to hear, loud enough to make Louie jump and stare: "Why don't you just go fuck yourself?"

The words echoed and disappeared, leaving the diner quieter than it had been all day. The fan over the grill hummed. The stereo in the dining room murmured a news report. The customers seemed to have frozen. I glared and Louie stared back, and neither of us moved.

Then his face exploded. He laughed so hard he fell to his knees and gasped for breath, wiping his eyes with the corner of his stained apron. I set about stacking plates and tossing silverware into a soapy bin, because what else could I do with this impossible man, this lunatic? Eventually Louie caught his breath, stood up, and put his arm around me, laughing and shaking his head and patting my arm. "You're a good girl," he said softly. "You're OK."

Diners are designed to bridge the gap between estrangement and community, to accommodate people both alone and in groups. Waiting on the counter was very different from waiting on tables, where I was careful to minimize interruptions into conversations (especially those between a middle-aged man and younger woman who arrived in separate cars and sat away from the windows, holding hands and gazing into each other's eyes). At the counter, strangers sat side-by-side and either maintained an imaginary boundary or crossed it with small talk of the sort that often involved me. Depending on the day and the customer, I was the joker, the sympathetic ear, the reflection back of the selves people hoped others might see. I didn't like my job, but there was satisfaction in being the person other people were so often glad to greet.

Every Saturday, from 6 a.m. until 4 p.m., Louie and I did our dance. "Stop yelling," I'd growl, and he'd look me straight in the eye. "Stop being so dumbass." If we happened to be behind the counter at that point, rather than in the kitchen, the regular customers within earshot laughed at the banter.

Most weeks each of my parents came into the diner and the counter worked its magic. When my mother left my father the second time, I hadn't really wanted to stay with him. My father was a familiar stranger, someone with a theoretical interest in me but not someone I could share much with apart from the occasional TV show. But when my mother announced she was leaving again, I knew that if I went with her, we'd be right back where we started, with a custody battle looming. Staying with my father appeased him while also allowing me to take a stand against her bad decisions.

Now, three years later, my father and I had arrived at a truce without the battle. We interacted more on Saturdays at the diner than during the rest of the week, and I preferred it that way. With the counter between us, I could float an idea—"There's a party at my friend Laura's house next Friday"—walk away while that much settled in, then return to ask if I could go. My father did the same thing. "I might not be home when you get in tonight," he'd say, and when I came back to refill his coffee cup, he'd add, "That all right with you?"

Things were a little different with my mother. She waited until the breakfast rush died down, and if my father's car was in the parking lot, she kept going and returned later. She often came in alone, and when I asked what she was up to that day, she shrugged and said something to the effect of, "Heading back home, I guess. She's got some party we're supposed to go to later." This was the same way she'd talked about my father, using a pronoun instead of a name, implying that someone else was in control.

"If you don't want to go, don't go," I snapped, shaking my head and walking away long enough for the sting to dissipate. Later I felt bad, and by the next week when she walked through the door, I was happy to see her again.

In this way the diner was a good thing, even though the only happy time of the week was Saturday night, when Monica borrowed her mother's car and we went to the mall to look for clothes and jewelry and cute guys. By Sunday morning, dread settled like fingers around my throat, and as the days inched nearer to my early-morning start time, I became more agitated, had a harder time sleeping. My dreams filled with customers, with tables I couldn't get to, plates of food I couldn't recognize, and Louie's incessant harping.

I thought often about quitting my job but didn't in part because I saw some truth in Louie's insults: I was, to a certain extent blind, to a certain extent stupid. There was so much I didn't know, about working efficiently and learning to forgive and appreciating people despite their flaws. And then there was the money, more money than I could have made anywhere else at that time, money that meant I didn't have to watch my father's forehead wrinkle as he opened his wallet to hand me some bills. But regardless of how seductive the tips were, I wouldn't have continued working those long, hard Saturday shifts if the evenings hadn't come along to balance them.

It turned out that Louie and Shirley had gotten married so he could stay in the country when his tourist visa ran out. The story they both told was that it had been a business deal, but the story I got from watching them was that Shirley had grown to love the man she called "that miserable bastard." They had opened the diner together, fulfilling his dream, and after a few months of financial struggle, Shirley had returned to her old job in a large, stainless-steel diner, where tips were more plentiful. Not long after that, they got the planned divorce, although Shirley continued to help out whenever Louie needed her.

One result of Shirley's leaving was that I got hired for Saturdays. Another, no surprise, was a rapid turnover of waitresses during the week. About a month into my career, Louie needed someone twice a week to cover the odd hours, from six in the evening, when the fiercely pretty waitress had to leave, until the diner closed at eight. I said yes to those mini-shifts because I thought they would give me practice for Saturday's hell. But almost no one came in. No one, that is, except my mother and brother and, sometimes, my father.

By then it was early June, the air fragrant and warm. Louie propped the front door open and I spent most of the time sitting at a table, reading the newspaper and drinking free Tab. When my mother and Michael came in, I jumped up and ran behind the counter, serving them with exaggerated gestures. Since I made no tips during those hours, except the fifty cents my mother would leave, Louie didn't bug me to clean or re-stock for the morning shift. He just let me lean on the counter and shoot the breeze with people who seemed more familiar here than anywhere else.

Michael was fourteen, a mop-topped eighth grader. We traded stories about teachers and commiserated about the uselessness of gym class, while my mother laughed and asked us questions. With the diner empty, I loosened up. I danced, cracked jokes, didn't flinch when Louie fired off an insult. When he went back in the kitchen, I rolled my eyes, and my mother laughed and called him pitiful. I found myself scanning through the days since I'd last seen her, looking for stories to share, ways of making her more a part of my life.

One day my mother confided that things had run their course with Jan, so she and Michael would be moving in with a new roommate, Sue, as soon as they found a place. Soon Sue began stopping in as well, motorcycle helmet in hand, her lanky frame leaning against the counter as she drank a Coke and talked, getting to know me. Shortly after, she and my mother found a house just down the road, and the diner became not only neutral territory but a geographical midpoint between our homes. Then it became more. When school ended, Louie hired Michael to sweep up at night and, as summer progressed, to wash dishes in the afternoon. I took on more evening hours, and more customers came in. My best friend stopped by frequently, and later, when she got fired from Burger King for flipping off the manager, Louie would hire the second worst waitress he'd ever seen.

That summer, the more time I spent with Louie, the more comfortable I became with his accent. One day he confessed that he often spoke quickly to confuse people, and that he threw in Greek words now and then, sometimes calling customers assholes, or worse, while they thanked him and wished his business well. He laughed himself silly telling me about it, and when I pronounced him the most disgusting person I'd ever met, he laughed even harder.

As the months wore on, I noticed how often Louie's eyes were bloodshot with exhaustion after twelve or fourteen hours on his feet, and I stopped complaining about my long hours on Saturday, which was a short day for him. Some evenings I'd find him asleep in a lawn chair outside the back door, and I'd leave him there and cook the hamburgers myself. In turn, Louie's demeanor changed. He'd curse at me or my brother for some small oversight, and five minutes later he'd tell us to taste the rice pudding, see how it came out, have a big dish of it if we wanted. "Here, *mouni*," he'd say to me, his voice soft with affection (even though the term he insisted meant *girl* is actually vulgar slang). For these small shifts in Louie's attitude and my own, I continued to work at the diner.

And for this, too: Some evenings that summer my mother and my father wandered into the diner at the same time. They sat a comfortable distance apart at the counter, three or four stools between them, and I held my breath until they passed some small talk. Then I gave a thumbs-up to Michael in the kitchen, and he came out, broom in hand, while Louie followed, moaning about how we were infesting the place, taking it over, running him out of town, and my parents shook their heads at what they couldn't understand.

On those evenings, I felt keenly the magical power of the American diner, with its public yet intimate space, its business of comfort, its mediation of loneliness. Moving between my mother and the kitchen, my father and the kitchen, bringing sandwiches and French fries and coffee to each of them, I appreciated this terrible job, along with the breeze blowing through the propped open door and the people who were almost, if not quite, a family.

HOW TO TELL A TRUE
LOVE STORY

Start with the time you both got drunk and slapped each other. "So there!" he said, palm smacking your cheek. "So there!" you retorted, whapping his forehead so hard he stumbled. It was 2:00 in the morning in a seaside town, the street lined with one-bedroom cottages. He got up and smacked your cheek again, making your head snap to the side. You didn't try to stop him, just waited your turn and walloped his forehead. It went on like that until a dim face appeared in the window of the cottage you were standing in front of and a young man's voice hissed, "Knock it off!" through the screen.

It's OK if that's not the way it happened, if the slapping wasn't really between you and him but between you and your best teenaged friend on summer vacation. The point here is to tell a good story, to catch the reader's attention straight away. So what if you never exchanged physical blows? Glowering can feel just as violent.

Or maybe you should start with something edgier, something with a clearer angle. A friend of mine, a best-selling author, insists that if you're writing from personal experience, you have to have a big story. Like your father was a spy. Or you climbed a snow-covered mountain and nearly died. Or you witnessed a war. If your love story happened during wartime, just outside Baghdad's green zone or, better yet, in the coca fields of Colombia, you're golden. Unless it involves the Vietnam War, which is passé, done to death. If your love story happened in 1971, don't even bother.

Something unique. That's what you've got to establish early on, that this love story is not like all the other love stories floating around in the world. But the problem with love stories is that they have only two outcomes: happiness or sadness. The love works out or the love does not, which is why you need the war or the mountain or the espionage, according to my friend.

Late September. Early evening. A cottage beside the Hudson River. There's a crowd of university people, hippy academics with guitars and hand-rolled cigarettes, and a beach covered with stones. Professor Wallace comes out in his swim trunks and tee shirt, his limbs pale and soft, and climbs into a kayak. You stand on the stones watching him paddle, everyone doubling over as the kayak shoots forward twenty feet before the waves carry him back, over and over again.

Not far away stands the guy, a lime floating in the plastic glass he holds aloft. "You can do it!" he shouts, one slim hip cocked. When you arrived at this party, wearing harem pants and a sleeveless turtleneck, his eyes had scanned in exactly the way you'd imagined while getting dressed. Now, as Professor Wallace paddles with everything he's got, guffawing as the oars splash water into his own face, you can feel the guy keeping an eye on you. Turn and walk up the stairs of the screened-in porch. Pop an oyster cracker into your mouth, scrutinize the liquor table. In half a minute, the door will creak. Don't turn around. Stand there for a moment, in this time just before dusk, with the laughter and the splashing and the slap of waves as an oil barge sends its wake to shore, with the cool evening air skimming the salt from your neck and Billie Holiday singing about the awful things love will make you do.

By the end of the night, he'll be drunk. You'll be drunk. Professor Wallace will be very drunk and singing "Peggy Sue" at the top of his lungs. The other professors will sing along and the grad students, too, and this will seem like exactly the life you were made for.

When the party is over, offer to give him a ride home. He'll grab two bottles of beer for the walk back to the car, along a path that leads through woods, through a meadow, over a stream to a grassy parking area. You've had quite a lot to drink, but you take the beer anyway because, drunk or sober, you're the best driver you know.

Before getting in the car, he takes hold of your elbow, gently, and turns you toward him. "Listen," he says. "Seriously. Can you get us home?"

You look up at the half-moon, casting its romantic light over the field. "We'll see," you tell him, and he kisses you hard, as if to say you're worth the risk.

OK, that's good. A little sexual tension, a bit of danger from the drinking and driving. But, you might ask, why not put the kiss somewhere else? Why not put it where it really happened, two weeks after the party by the river, on the street in front of his house? And not a hard kiss at all, but a kiss so soft you could feel it for days? Because a true love story has to have a kiss early on, that's why. Otherwise what's the purpose of the cabin on the river? Why leave poor Professor Wallace stuck out in that kayak for half an hour, damp tee shirt clinging to his skin? The kiss gets things going, sets the primary conflict in motion. Just be careful not to lose track of the bigger story, the angle, the hook.

You drink because you like to drink. You like the taste of whiskey, the fuzzy tongue of it licking your lips. You like to feel your edges soften and hear words come out of your mouth in an order that sounds like insight. You like to feel convinced of all the potential that lies ahead.

He drinks for a different reason, or maybe it's the same reason intensified. Beer, wine, whiskey, gin, he moves from one to the other in a single evening, trying to mitigate the stream of darkness that leaks from his cerebral cortex, drains along his spinal cord, pools in his small intestine. He has poison inside him, a persistent sense of worthlessness that alcohol dilutes. When he drinks, you soon discover, he's a funnier, kinder, more entertaining version of himself.

But be careful here. Don't get caught up in the alcohol because that angle has really been done. No one will care that he stopped drinking out of the blue, claiming to be an alcoholic, or that you didn't believe it, having known serious drunks in your life. "Get over yourself," you said, ordering a Maker's Mark straight up.

Skip the months of depression, too. The dirty end of winter and tender spring, apple blossoms turning the air so thick it was sometimes hard to see while driving. Cut to Mother's Day, when he used a razor blade to make long, deep cuts in one arm. But that part's a drag to write, so don't linger. Does the world really need another description of blood on the floor, another emergency room scene with a social worker explaining a cry for help?

Be advised: your agent, real or imagined, won't like this. "You're skirting the important part," he'll say, and even if you manage to convince him, there will be the editor, the marketing person, the aim to have it shelved somewhere lucrative. "Grief and Recovery," maybe. Or "Self-help." They'll want you to keep thinking of the big story, the angle, the hook.

But attempted suicide is not a hook, I can tell you. Who doesn't take too many pills once in a while? Who hasn't held a razor blade against their skin, drawn a little blood? It's not the attempt that matters, it's the result. And the result was something you never could have imagined. He lived, and you fell in love. On that day in the emergency room, the thighs of his jeans stiff with blood, the disappointment in his eyes each time he looked at you — "I can't even kill myself right," he'd scoffed — you didn't see the romance coming, didn't understand how after intense drama, the heart circles its wagons, hunkers down, refuses to let go.

You hadn't yet heard of the shaky bridge experiment, in which male subjects were enlisted to walk across two suspension bridges in a forest. One bridge was sturdy and low to the ground while the other swayed hundreds of feet in the air, with low rails and a genuine element of danger. After each subject crossed whichever bridge he'd been assigned, an attractive female member of the research team offered her phone number in case he had questions later about the experiment. The result? Guys who walked across the scary bridge were almost 50%

more likely not just to call the woman but to ask her out on a date. The emotional aftermath of danger often feels like romance.

You'll want to use a scene to illustrate this, to capture the appeal of a guy who comes home from the hospital still bandaged. But watch out for clichés, for sentimentality, for the stale confines of truth. In *The Lifespan of a Fact*, John D'Agata explains why he changed some details in an essay he'd written about a teenaged boy's suicide in Las Vegas, including small, insignificant details, like the number of strip clubs in that city. There were thirty-one at the time of the suicide, and he made it thirty-four because, he says, "the rhythm of 'thirty-four' works better in that sentence than the rhythm of 'thirty-one.'" Never mind that you can't hear the difference, never mind the troubling idea that reality needs to be enhanced to make a good story. The story is what matters most. So play around with form and content, give yourself permission, do what you need to do.

Write the scene. Write how one day you're a graduate student fretting over final exams, with a boyfriend who might not be worth the trouble after all, and two weeks later, the sun shines in Technicolor, the creek outside your window erupts in a blaze of diamonds each time a carp jumps. He walks through the door, left forearm dressed from wrist to elbow, a little thinner from the hospital food but otherwise himself. Short dark hair, bright green eyes, walking straight to the living room window overlooking the creek. "Seen that big fish lately?" he asks, and your heart swells because he's back. But the window is three stories up, a small balcony on the other side of it, and you're not sure how you'll sleep that night without nailing the window shut.

"Two weeks, start to finish," he says the next day. "That's a pretty efficient recovery from a full mental breakdown."

But of course he isn't recovered. That's what the agent, real or imagined, will have a hard time seeing, and the editor and the marketing person. That's the cliché you have to guard against, no matter how much you want to hook the reader. In a true love story, as in so many other stories, recovery is beside the point.

A true love story is always messy. A mutual friend once said to you, "Life with him will always be tough. Now it's depression, and later it will be something else." You ended that friendship right quick. Who needs such negativity, even if there is wisdom in the words, even if you received them like a prophecy?

It's true that those words contributed, eventually, to your decision to break up with him, but listen, breakups aren't that interesting either, so unless you're in Baghdad's green zone or the coca fields of Colombia, get through that part quickly. Focus instead on the aftermath, on the friendship you forged. Years, it took, for the sense of betrayal on both sides to settle, for the dissipation of anger at how life follows its own path, regardless of what you want. And then there you were, closer than some siblings. You talked on the phone every few weeks, met up for dinner in Manhattan, visited each other, him flying to the Midwest, you driving to Long Island, where you spent one New Year's Eve celebrating with his coworkers, including a woman who refused to believe you wouldn't reconcile. Why couldn't you move to Sag Harbor, she wanted to know. Or spend the summer at least. "You two," she moaned, shaking her head.

Because in a true love story, the romance lives on. In a true love story, you can act like a couple, eating off each other's plates, bantering, rehearsing anecdotes that show you each in good and bad lights, then walk to the car arm in arm because the rancor is gone and in its place pure appreciation. The woman on New Year's Eve didn't see the waves he rode, the new relationships he burned, or hear the phone calls when he was in a bad state. "Are you seeing a therapist?" you sometimes asked, and he responded, "Yeah," or "Nope," or "For all the fucking good it does." The woman didn't know about the anti-depressants, the lithium, the way he drank socially, quite a lot sometimes, then announced he'd quit again and that was when you worried.

On the other hand, maybe post-love romance, the kind of romance you felt that New Year's Eve and on the other visits and during the phone chats when he sounded like himself and called you "Sweetie," isn't all that interesting, either. It might be if you'd slept together now and then in a sexual way, not just in the way of that winter night when you both wore sweatpants and long-sleeved shirts and curled back-to-back in his unheated beach house. There's no tension to the pillow talk of thirty-something exes, no thrill to waking at 3 a.m. and thinking, "We did it. We're in this for the long haul." Such satisfaction, such belief in the happy ending. And where does that get you?

Your agent and editor, real or imagined, will want the story to move ahead, summarizing the friendship part and getting to the last phone call, the familiar sound of sarcasm. You'd always been able to talk him out of those moods, to chip away with your rigorous sense of logic until light came through the thatched roof of disappointment under which he lived. But this time was different. This time it had to do with money, with the stock market crashing, with the fact that he'd resigned from his teaching job and gone back to school, believing himself to be wealthy, and now the money was turning into smoke. Floating away. Of course you'd said this all along: the money isn't real. When the value of his beach house skyrocketed, you were the one who pointed out that value doesn't equal money until you sell. So he sold and moved to a cheaper area and invested, and when the returns came in, he called and thanked you for the great advice, even though you hadn't thought he should sell at all, just that he shouldn't consider himself rich.

When the bottom fell out, he lamented, "Everything will be gone soon," and you replied, for perhaps the hundredth time, "That's crazy talk." You insisted the market would come back, even if it took a while, but you were also tired, impatient. You heard entitlement in his voice, and only later, replaying the conversation over and over in your mind, would you hear despair.

A true love story contains heartache. Always. Loss or potential loss or a past that's brighter than the future. But the agent, real or imagined, is right. The editor is right. The marketing person knows what she's doing. No one wants your sorry story unless it ends with redemption. So find yourself a happy ending. Dig around in reality, in the disconnected phone line and the missing person's report, in the call to his sister, who told you about the note, the copy of the will mailed to his parents. Look past the months before a hiker came upon what the papers called "remains," the way his picture flashed across the news feed and the dreams you had for a long time after, in which he visited you from the beyond or you visited him in the beyond and he wasn't always happy to see you. That's not the way the story is supposed to go, with no closure, no lesson learned. Remember that a story, true or false or some combination of the two, is a made thing. Make it.

And if you can't do that, if you can't find an ending that's happy or at least resolved or that points toward something positive for readers to grasp onto, and if you also can't make your peace with changing reality to fit your narrative, then maybe you're on your way to telling the truest love story there is. Just know it probably won't sell. Because a really true love story ends not with tears or guilt or reconciliation but with the simple acknowledgment that your life is a good one, that despite the constant see-saw of loss and gain, you're grateful every day to be here.

And yet. You miss the after-romance, that long period like love but different, the sense of optimism that won't entirely go away, even now. You keep trying to tell the story from a fresh angle, find the slant that brings everything to light, warp the years enough to hear his voice resonating from a thousand miles away, but it doesn't work. There is nothing new to say. Only the ending remains, and even that isn't original, it's the ending you were headed toward all along, the ending of every true love story ever told: life goes on.

RESTLESS

In the early 1980s, when we were still stunned, still thinking it was a big-city thing, a faraway thing, not a Metro-
North Hudson Line thing, David wasted away. We knew
as soon as he couldn't kick colds, as soon as his smoker's
cough intensified, because it would have taken fortune
greater than anything we believed in to protect someone
with that lust for life, that lust for any man walking down
the street in tight blue jeans and cowboy boots.

   Before all that, there was the time when David cat-
called a guy from his car, on my mother's block at 11:00 at
night, and the guy charged toward him screaming threats,
forcing David to drive around for a while before parking and running like hell to the second-floor apartment.
By then we thought he might not show up. We'd started
cooking, my mother and her ex-girlfriend Sue, who lived
in the spare bedroom, and Michael, a sophomore in high
school, and me, the nineteen-year-old who didn't live
there but sometimes slept on the couch. That Friday evening my mother, Sue, David and a passel of their friends

had gone to happy hour after work, and my brother and I had watched movies until we each fell asleep—him on the couch and me in the recliner. When my mother and Sue burst in laughing a little before 11 p.m., I got up, intending to go home.

But Sue was hungry and David was on his way, so my mother pulled out a package of pork chops and Sue started slicing onions and their laughter lured us into the kitchen. I peeled potatoes while Michael cracked a dozen eggs into a bowl. By the time David burst in, indignant and shaking, a breakfast-dinner was sizzling. "He called me a cocksucker!" David yelled, and there was a three-second pause before he added, "And he doesn't even know me!" and the rest of us doubled over, laughing so hard we cried, and David cried, too, because how could he not?

How could he not? David was a nut, my mother always said, in the affectionate way she described anyone who made her laugh. He was handsome and flirtatious, a man who would sling an arm around my shoulders and comment on the way a blouse hugged my breasts without wanting anything in return. That night he was drunk, the way everyone was always mildly drunk and driving home because home wasn't too far away and the speed limit on city streets just 30mph. But he was also afraid, the first time I'd seen him wide-eyed and shaking.

David didn't relax until we started eating, and then he settled into telling stories in his usual, animated way. There was the time his mother chased him down the street toward the bus stop, demanding he change that ridiculous shirt, the time he took a nap at his office desk, snoring so loud the boss heard him down the hall. We laughed and licked our fingers, the pork chops juicy, potatoes fried crisp, eggs scrambled with peppers and onions and plenty of salt, all of it so delicious we ate second helpings and thirds, until it was gone and David and Sue and my mother were sober again. They yawned and stretched, stubbed out cigarettes, talked about what the rest of the weekend might hold. Sue said, "You're going back to the bar tonight, aren't you?" and David said, "Are you crazy?" and Sue said, "Bullshit," and we all laughed.

It was 1:00 in the morning by then, and I felt full and awake. Restless. Not restless like David, who kept shifting in his chair and opening his mouth as if to speak, but restless in the way of early adulthood, when you want something you can't name, something that takes you out into the world and casts your life into flattering relief.

"I'll go with you," I said, wanting to get up and move and feel the night air on my skin. "Come on, let's go dancing."

David raised his eyebrows at my mother as if to say, "Should I take her to the gay bar in the rough area of town?" My mother shrugged, knowing that David wanted to go out just long enough to go back in again, someone else in tow, and I wasn't that person.

But I couldn't bear the idea that a Friday night injected with all this energy could revert to its dull self, so I turned to Michael, sixteen years old and as awake as I was. "How about you and I go to a bar?"

His eyes widened as he sat up straight and tried to play it cool. "I mean, I guess. If you really want to."

"They won't card us at this hour, right?" I asked. David said nah, Sue said they might, and my mother shrugged again. "If it doesn't work out, just come back home."

I drove us to a small bar near the community college I attended, the kind of bar people stopped at on their way to or from somewhere else. Michael tried to look calm as we entered, shifting his glance left and right, while my own glance went immediately to the pool table, where two high school friends, John and Scott, were playing. I hadn't seen them in almost two years, not since I'd dated them both, in a way, along with my friend Monica, who'd gotten her driver's license before anyone else. Her parents used to let us borrow their car as long as we promised not to allow others into it, and we did promise, of course, on those Friday nights before we picked up Scott and John and headed to the liquor store and then the drive-in movie theater and then a spot along the Hudson River where we wouldn't be seen. There we did shots and danced by the water's edge and riffed off each other, laughing until we couldn't breathe. John and Scott both had girlfriends, popular girlfriends, and we all worried about them finding out because, as Scott once said, the only thing worse than being cheated on for sex was being cheated on for fun.

Now, John and Scott greeted me with open arms, each of them a little broader, a little fuller in the face. John ordered a pitcher of beer and four glasses, no questions asked, and we sat down at a table and drained the pitcher a few times. The three of us reminisced about that crazy romance without the romance we'd all had, and my brother cracked us up with imitations of the teachers he was still dealing with, and before long the bar was closing at 4 a.m.

We talked a while longer in the parking lot. Eventually Michael shook hands with the guys and I hugged each of them, long hugs tight with the possibility of never seeing one another again. Then, mildly drunk, I drove back to the second-story apartment where my mother slept in the big bedroom and Sue slept in the middle bedroom and my brother headed to his small bedroom off the kitchen. My father's house was only two miles away, but that seemed so far I kicked off my shoes and stretched out on the couch.

How happy I felt lying there, aware of the thin tethers connecting us all. I thought about the desire that filled the car on those secretive Friday nights with Scott and John and Monica and about how we never acted on it, any of us, because desire itself was what we were after. I thought about my current boyfriend, off hunting that weekend, even though he didn't like killing deer, because what he loved most was to get up early in the morning, climb into a tree, get high, and enjoy the woods. I thought about sweet, crazy David, always laughing, always game, always on the make, David who called a great ass when he saw one, no matter who it belonged to, and who, I didn't know then, had just two more years before his immune system collapsed. I thought about Sue, who seemed to be in love with my mother still, and about my mother, who had passed the belief on to me for safekeeping, even though she would later lose sight of it herself, that it was OK to be whoever you were and experiment however you might because God loved all his children, even the ones who drank too much and ate too much and couldn't help wanting what they wanted and sometimes getting it, and then wanting more and getting that, too. If they were lucky.

If we were lucky.

All of us.

In that time before.

ALL THE POWER
THIS CHARM DOTH OWE

For more than a year we'd noticed each other around town. I was drawn to his Irish face, the eyes that crinkled when he smiled, the smile itself. I liked that he spent hours reading in coffee shops and said hello to people as if he were glad to see them. But we didn't know each other.

Through most of that year, I'd been trying not to become involved with a married man. My resolve had been strong in the beginning, but the married man was charming and cool in his crisp white tee shirt, hipster glasses, Louisiana drawl hanging on for dear life. I liked the way he laughed and danced and asked questions, then listened to the answers. In the college town where I was nearing the end of graduate school, the married man owned a popular restaurant, so everybody knew him and everybody liked him, and now and then when he stopped by my house smelling like cardamom, I got tired of taking the high road.

In other words, there was drama in my life, the way there often is in the lives of people who reach their mid-thirties without the grounding force of career or relationship. I would let the married man hang out for half an hour, flattered by his compliments and maybe giving in to some kissing and pressing against one another, and then I'd come to my senses and send him away. Later, on a walk downtown, I might pass the guy with the Irish face and when he smiled and nodded hello, I wondered if the moment of calm I felt right then was worth more than reckless passion. What good ever came of being swept off your feet, beyond the initial dopamine thrill? Why not aim instead for someone solid and stable and maybe even available?

We met on one of those steel-gray January mornings with a wind that had blown down from the Rockies and gathered strength across the Plains before skimming the icy Iowa River and scraping our cheeks raw. In the campus writing center where I was a tutor and he a tutor-in-training, we unwrapped ourselves, shedding gloves and scarves and hats and parkas, smiling. His name was Kevin. He was working on a PhD in American Studies. He'd started grad school two years after I did, so his comprehensive exams were coming up at the end of the term. I was working on my dissertation, but before we had a chance to say more, the first students arrived.

Over the next months, during our twice-a-week shifts, Kevin and I took each other's measure. On busy days there was time only to say hello, and on other days we might chat for ten or fifteen minutes, slowly getting to know each other. He was from Massachusetts. Active in the graduate student union. A voracious reader but not, thank goodness, a writer. He seemed smart, funny, sane. I began to imagine him as my next serious boyfriend, even though neither of us made a move.

Meanwhile, the married man continued to pursue things until the middle of the term, when I decided to employ tough love by going out with a friend of his. The friend was older, attractive, wealthy, and a Republican, which might have been a deal-breaker except he'd grown up in Birmingham during the civil rights era, a product of the Black Power movement, so he understood some things. And, of course, dating him would render me off-limits to the married man. For a month the friend and I enjoyed a comfortably physical relationship and then, having almost nothing in common, we let more and more time pass before returning each other's calls. It was the perfect, short fling, after which we chatted amiably when we ran into each other on the street, with no mention of getting together again. As planned, the married man relegated me to the friend zone.

Through all of this, twice a week there was Kevin. We talked in short spurts about growing up on the east coast and about how out of place our sarcasm sometimes felt in Iowa. We talked about the courses we'd taken and the courses we taught, about books and movies and where we hoped to live after grad school, and over time our conversations took on the tenor not of flirting, exactly, but of companionable checking in. I began to imagine that after he finished his exams, we would go on our first date, and after that we would spend a relaxing summer getting to know each other, and after that, who knew? A whole lifetime, perhaps.

As the term drew to a close, I could see only one wrinkle to this plan: my mother was coming to town.

The previous summer, my mother had visited Iowa for the first time, stopping over on her annual trip to Las Vegas, where my brother lived. When she asked whether I was seeing anyone, I decided to be honest and told her about the married man, which made her eyebrows pinch together. That changed when we had breakfast at his restaurant and he came out of the kitchen to shake my mother's hand and offer observations about her height ("Those are some seriously long legs") and her eyes ("That's like a cornflower blue, right?") and her astrology sign ("Leo? So you're fierce"). In his presence she beamed like a child. We barely got out the door before she shook her head, hand on her heart, and said, "Good luck with that one."

My mother understood better than anyone the kind of attraction that sneaks up and grabs you, regardless of what you think you want. Her first girlfriend had offered that and more, appreciating and doting on her. When that relationship frayed after a few years, another woman came immediately onto the scene, and after her a series of men. There was the fire chief I learned about when a police scanner appeared beside my mother's bed, crackling through the night so she'd know when he was in danger. There was the man who prepared elaborate Italian meals for her but often drank so much while cooking that he fell asleep at the table. After him there was a patient at the psychiatric hospital where she worked, a guy my brother's age, with whom she often spent Friday evenings playing board games on the locked ward. My mother knew how people talked about her, the woman from housekeeping who worked all day changing beds and cleaning bathrooms only to come back at night for a guy half her age, and said she didn't care. It was a free country and she could be friends with anyone she wanted. Once when I visited her during winter break, the guy's voice came through her telephone answering machine in a languid stream of honeys and sweethearts. "What a nut," my mother laughed, shaking her head as if to hide the blush in her cheeks. For a while she even dyed her hair again.

These days my mother was unattached, as far as I knew, and returning to Iowa because of a crisis: the physical labor of her job, of mopping and scouring all day, had taken a toll on her back. Although she was just sixty-two years old, her doctor had consigned her to disability retirement. On the day she got the news, she phoned me in tears and I pictured her elbows resting on the kitchen table in Poughkeepsie, New York, one hand on the phone and the other holding her forehead framed by silver hair. As a state employee, she would receive a decent retirement package, but filling time was something else, as was feeling that she made a small difference in other people's lives. "What am I going to *do* with myself?" she cried.

"Come visit me," I responded. I was thinking that retirement is hard enough when you see it coming and have time to prepare, let alone when your kids live in different time zones and your closest friends have started to move to Florida and even die. I wanted to console my mother, to seduce her into believing that the future was filled with possibility. "Let me take care of you for a few days," I said, imagining the meals I'd prepare, the massage I would schedule, the way being tended to might help her recharge and pivot in a new direction.

My mother sniffed and sighed and said she'd think about it, and we hung up. Half an hour later she called again, her voice lighter. She had just booked a flight. She would arrive the day after I gave my last final exam. And the best part, she said as if offering a gift, was that she would stay for two whole weeks.

That spring I was teaching an Introduction to Literature class that included Shakespeare's *A Midsummer Night's Dream*. Even the most resistant students ended up enjoying the humor of a play in which romance flourishes deep in the forest, where members of the fairy world play tricks on humans and each other. Under the influence of magical love potions, couples form and re-form, including Tatiana the fairy queen and Nick Bottom, a blustery laborer whose head has turned into a donkey's. Love, the play demonstrates, makes fools of us all.

That's how I felt on the last day of spring classes: foolish. By then I'd developed a full-blown crush on Kevin and thought he might feel the same way about me, and I expected that before we left work, we'd make plans to see each other again. But when our shift ended, Kevin headed for the door, waving goodbye with his usual, good-natured smile.

That evening, over pizza with friends at a restaurant in town, I whined about not being able to trust my own intuition. I never assumed someone was interested in me, but this time there had been signs. Or so I thought. My friends shook their heads, puzzled by all this distress over a guy I'd never mentioned. Later, walking home alone, I paused on the bridge over Ralston Creek and inhaled the summer scent of flowers and weeds and roots and tree bark, a smell that made me feel six years old again, playing by myself at the edge of the yard where pricker bushes gave home to spiders and beetles, whole communities going about their business with no regard for my existence. Aloneness swelled in my gut and seemed to infuse not just that evening but the future stretching ahead. Maybe I'd exhausted my allotment of romantic love already. Maybe, like my mother, I would age on my own, but without the consolation of kids who checked in regularly and visited a couple times a year.

A few blocks farther I turned onto my street and came to the small, wood-frame house where my apartment occupied half of the first floor. I'd lived there for five years, my most permanent adult address by far, and liked coming home to the front porch shaded by a lilac tree and decorated with the table and chairs I'd found at a yard sale. A single woman lived in each of the three apartments inside, and I enjoyed that proximity, the way sounds seeped through the walls and floors. I knew when Cynthia positioned her easel on the hardwood floor above my living room, or when Annie's girlfriend was in town, her staccato hums seeping through a shared bedroom wall. My apartment was tiny, with uneven floors and not much closet space, but the layout was nice, allowing sun to shine through windows on three sides of the building, including onto a window seat in the living room where my cats often slept. That's where they were on this night in early May, both of them jumping down when I entered and following me along the hall from the living room, past the kitchen and bathroom to the bedroom, where the red light of an answering machine winked.

In an instant, everything made sense. Of course Kevin wouldn't ask me out at work. Of course he would find my number on his own and call me at home. Of course he was a thoughtful, responsible, grown-up man. I'd known it all along.

I called him back and we met for a drink that night, after which he walked me to the corner of my street and said a polite goodbye. A few nights later we had dinner, and a few nights after that dinner again. On that third date, after he walked me home, we sat in the living room drinking beer. He had an intriguing combination of a quiet demeanor and a sharp sense of humor, and I watched the way he played with my big orange cat, dangling a toy high enough so he'd leap, but not so high that he couldn't catch it. This was not, I thought, a man who teased.

But when he'd emptied his bottle of beer, Kevin thanked me and stood up. "I have a final exam to give in the morning," he said, and I thought, oh no. The narrative I'd been following, in which a couple gets to know one another slowly, their closeness progressing through old-fashioned courtship, became twisted like the branch of a gnarled tree, new limbs splitting into possibilities I hadn't seen coming. He wasn't interested anymore. I'd said something that turned him off. He liked me but felt no physical attraction. He was a closeted gay man trying to find a woman he could settle for. He was a straight man with a fear of intimacy.

In the split second it took for these interpretations to unfurl, Kevin turned and asked whether I'd been thinking of the evening as a date. My face burned with the seventh-grade mortification of liking someone who might not like me *in that way*, but he held my gaze until I admitted that yes, I'd assumed so. "Me, too," he said, hazel eyes crinkling. Then he kissed me as if stating his intentions, hands on my upper arms, lips pressed momentarily against mine. When the door closed and his footsteps bounced off the porch, I fell onto the couch, laughing.

As passengers appeared in the gate area of the Cedar Rapids airport, greeting loved ones or striding toward baggage claim, I gave myself a talking to: Be patient. Be nice. She's going through a hard time right now. Make her feel loved.

Then my mother was in front of me, blue eyes searching, and the miracle of flight once again took my breath away. When she saw me, she began to smile before pulling her bright pink lips into a frown. "Any tornadoes in the forecast this time?" she cracked.

During her visit the previous summer, we'd had a flat-line windstorm so intense it triggered tornado sirens and sent balls of hail through plastic lawn furniture. We'd spent the storm in the basement with my friend Becky, who bounded down the stairs with a guy from her soft-ball team after the windshield of his van shattered as they were driving past. Annie was there, too, and Cynthia came down with a plate of nachos to share, and I thought that day showcased Iowa City at its best. When the storm ended, neighbors gathered on the street to survey dam-age and crack jokes, a hardy, resilient community I felt proud to call home. But my mother had been so fright-ened she vowed never to come back.

Now, as I leaned in for a hug, she said, "I almost died here last time."

"Not really," I sang, relieving her of a carry-on bag. "How does your back feel?"

She pursed her lips and shrugged. "I hope my first dis-ability check doesn't come while I'm not home. I don't want anything to happen to it."

We walked slowly. My mother really was all legs, long, thin legs that called to mind the person I remembered from childhood. She'd been slender and graceful then, her brown hair styled by permanent waves and rollers. One of my childhood pleasures had been staring at a news-paper clipping of her engagement to a man who wasn't my father, its photo taken when she was eighteen and her hair peroxide blonde. Her face was so full and smooth, so free of anxious furrows, that she seemed a familiar strang-er captured at the beginning of a happy story. Each time I looked at the photograph, I wished for a future in which that first fiancé didn't change his mind, didn't break her heart, even though my own existence depended on things working out exactly as they had.

Now my mother's soft face was deeply lined, her mid-section round, hair silver-gray in front and dark gray in back. There was a slight rocking motion when she walked, as if her feet were becoming rigid.

While we waited for her suitcase to appear on the conveyor belt, my mother relayed how early she'd gotten up that morning, how long it had taken her to get to the airport, the dollar amounts of each bill she'd paid the previous night. I listened, encouraging myself to nod and affirm, understand and validate and not, good God, snap at her to forget the minutiae of leaving home and just be here now.

She recognized the forced patience on my face. "You probably don't need me here taking up all your time," she said, and before I could protest, her tone turned accusatory: "What would you be doing right now if I wasn't here?"

I took a deep breath and thought of Kevin stopping by my place the night before on his way to a party. He'd invited me along, but I was busy cleaning and putting sheets on the bed and on the fold-out futon chair in the living room where I would sleep for the next two weeks, so we sat down on the couch, kissing for real and whispering about how bad the timing was. I'd already explained that I wouldn't see him during my mother's visit. "I'm not the best version of myself around her," I told him, and he assured me he understood.

If not for my mother's arrival, I thought, I would probably be in bed with him right now. Or maybe we'd have walked into town for breakfast on this lovely May morning, dizzy in the way that comes often at the beginnings of relationships. Part of me wanted that scenario to have played out, while another was content to take things slow, slower than anything I'd experienced before. We'd known each other more than four months, ten days had passed since our first date, and we still hadn't gotten past first base.

My smile was genuine, even as I lied to my mother, insisting that if she hadn't arrived, I would have spent the morning grading, and picking her up was much more fun. That settled her for a few minutes, but in the parking lot she wondered aloud if she ought to have stayed home and not disrupted my schedule. This was one of the many dynamics between us: she asked for reassurance that she was wanted and loved, and knowing it was impossible to provide enough, I side-stepped. Still, this trip had been my idea, and I really did want to ease her distress. "I'm glad you're here, Mom," I said, closing the trunk and unlocking the passenger's side door. "Really."

A light breeze carried the smell of baked oats from the Quaker factory in Cedar Rapids. Under a perfect dome of Midwestern sky, I felt a burst of excitement at the prospect of driving my mother back to my small, sunlit apartment and serving the quiche I'd made for lunch. At nearly thirty-five years old, I still took pleasure in showing her what I could do.

"How much is the parking?" she asked, reaching for her purse.

I grabbed four quarters from a nook in the dashboard. "I've got it right here."

"No, no. I'll pay," my mother insisted, as I coasted up to the parking attendant's window and said hello. Perhaps because she had lived through real poverty as a child, my mother balanced her checkbook down to the penny and paid back every dime she borrowed from anyone. I, on the other hand, was getting through school partly by using credit cards for auto repairs and even groceries at the end of each month, then paying what I could before transferring the balance to a new credit card with a 0% introductory interest rate. I'd effectively had an interest-free loan for three years and was not only proud of the scheme but impatient with my mother's ledgers.

I handed the quarters to the attendant.

"Here," my mother repeated, and I said, "I've got it, Mom," and she warned, "If you don't let me pay, I'll get right back on a plane and go home!"

My mother often made half-hearted threats at moments when she felt powerless and vulnerable. A decade before, while visiting her sister in Florida, she had made the same comment about getting back on a plane, and my aunt had replied in her perpetually even tone, "Suit yourself." My mother still told the story, angry as a shaved cat each time.

I couldn't resist. Stepping on the gas, lowering the visor against the morning sun, I shrugged and said, in the best imitation I could of my aunt's voice, "Suit yourself."

My mother gasped and swore and sputtered before launching once again into the story of that terrible visit with her sister, and by the time she finished we were both laughing. The ice had broken, the distance between us lessened. I imagined there would be more of these negotiations over the next two weeks, and not all of them would end well. But one consolation was that Kevin wouldn't witness them.

I missed him. Mid-afternoon found me sitting on the porch with a stack of final papers while my mother napped. She'd loved the quiche, dotted with shrimp and broccoli, and the salad, and the gift certificate for the massage, which I'd scheduled for the next afternoon. She'd been so happy about that appointment she hadn't even protested against my spending money on her.

The lilac tree's perfume was so sweet it bordered on repulsive, and I breathed it in over and over, trying to locate the exact moment when pleasure became too much. I scanned the sidewalk, north toward College Street and south to the corner of Burlington Avenue. Kevin had no reason to walk past, but I couldn't help hoping he would. Surely he missed me too, at the beginning of this ridiculous separation. Or maybe not. Maybe during these two weeks, he'd cool toward me. Or meet someone else. Anything could happen.

After my mother woke, we went for a long walk and chatted in that slow, luxurious way that only happens in person, when silence is filled in by all the stimuli you experience together, your bodies adjusting to each other's pace as you stop at street corners and start again after a car has passed. She asked about the married guy and I said that was finally over. "Good for you," she replied. "He was hard to resist." Then she asked if there was anybody else in the picture. I said kind of. A guy I'd gone out with a couple of times. She asked if she was going to meet him, and I said probably not, since I'd told him that I wanted to focus on her while she was here. She didn't protest and seemed flattered by being a priority in my life.

After dinner at a pizzeria in town, we strolled home in the soft evening air. Most undergraduates had cleared out by then, and Iowa City felt small, intimate. At the corner of Jefferson and Gilbert, we ran into my friend Liz, who hugged my mother and welcomed her back. Three blocks later we met Becky coming out of the grocery co-op and walked her home. What a gorgeous night, everyone kept saying, such a gorgeous night after such a terrible winter, and before the heat settles in. "You're here at the right time," Becky said, and my mother nodded before reminding her of last year's storm.

Back at home, I switched on a light in the pre-dusk living room and headed for the bedroom, my mother following. She slipped her sandals off and nudged them under the bed and was standing right beside me when I hit "play" on the answering machine and Kevin's voice filled the room: "Hey there. Hope you two are having a nice time so far. I was wondering if I could take you out for ice cream this evening. Let me know if you're up for it."

"What?" I said aloud, replaying the previous night's conversation, when Kevin assured me he understood why I wouldn't contact him during my mother's visit and said he looked forward to seeing me again in two weeks. What part of that hadn't he understood?

"Call him," my mother said, already wiggling her feet back into her sandals. "Ice cream sounds good to me."

First grade. Second grade. Third. On Saturday mornings, my mother and brother and I sometimes went shopping, combing department stores for sales on clothing and whatever odds and ends were needed that week: thread, wrapping paper, a pair of slippers. Mostly I loved those trips, the overfull clothing racks at Bradlee's, the popcorn-and-candy smells of Montgomery Ward, but on cold or wet days, especially in winter, my mother wore a polyester scarf over her hair, tied under the chin, and her favorite boots—black, ankle-height, rubber galoshes. The faux fur around the tops were meant to be decorative, but since she didn't zip the boots, the fur flopped around like the mouths of monsters swallowing her feet. In each store I noticed other women's feet encased in leather or quilted fabric or synthetic fur, with rubber wedge heels. Those women seemed ready for adventure, while my mother seemed ready to harvest potatoes. I spent a lot of time wandering the stores on my own, pretending not to know her.

Michael didn't share my embarrassment, maybe because he was a couple years younger or because he was a boy or because he was a better, less judgmental person. All these explanations came to mind as I moved into and through the teen years, my taste in almost everything developing in direct opposition to my mother's. I loathed country music, read classic literature, preferred the breathability of cotton to synthetic fabrics, became a feminist. My mother and I got along best during the latter part of her lesbian years, when her social life was filled with hilarious people bonded together by outsider status and her motto was "live and let live." But by the time I went away to college and she had worked for several years at the psychiatric hospital, she'd become more conservative and more coarse. Most of her friends now had no idea that she'd loved women or frequented gay bars in the past, and she used ethnic slurs with abandon, phrases like "dumb Polack" and "stubborn Guinea" and worse. When I asked her to stop she grew angry, insisting she meant nothing by it. "Oh, I wouldn't want to *embarrass* you," she said once in a checkout line where I'd rolled my eyes as several heads turned at her language. Later she would say with disappointment that college had changed me, which was true. But it was also true, although I'd have denied it to the death if she'd called me on it, that the chagrin I'd begun to show in college had been there all along.

Kevin came down the block, wearing blue plaid shorts and a navy tee shirt, sandals on his feet, a baseball cap highlighting his boyish face. "Hi there," he said, smiling, and my mother smiled back. She seemed surprised, relieved. Here was a normal guy, a guy who looked less like a fancy-pants academic than someone who might wander into her neighborhood bar. He wasn't dangerously charismatic like the married guy or pretentious like my last serious boyfriend. He was friendly. Comfortable. Asking questions about what we'd done that afternoon and, almost immediately, about my mother's injured back.

As we walked, I told Kevin how surprised I'd been to hear from him. He shrugged and smiled. "Everybody likes ice cream, right?" he said, winking as if we both understood that my plan had been ridiculous. Well, yes, I thought, but not everybody wants to introduce a new guy to the mother who might make him think twice about his dating choices.

The heart of Iowa City is a leafy, T-shaped pedestrian mall. We sat on one of its benches, ice cream in hand, the music from a live salsa band down the block rocking our feet and shoulders. Small children marched past, followed by their parents, and the occasional grad student waved hello. On the bench next to ours, two ped-mall regulars from the International Socialist Organization sat smoking hand-rolled cigarettes, and across Washington Street a dark-suited preacher stood next to a sandwich board proclaiming Jesus the savior. The preacher showed up every Friday night year-round, sometimes with his bonnet-headed wife and daughters, to shout condemnation at passers-by. We would all go to hell, he promised, if we didn't change our ways.

"Ain't he something?" my mother said with a chuckle. She leaned forward, looking past me to Kevin. "Hey, should we stand up and shout back? If you hold your hat out, we might collect some money." Kevin laughed, and I thought for the thousandth time: I'm too hard on her.

Later we strolled around the former state capitol building with its beaux-arts columns and gold dome shining against a purple sky and stood looking at the view across the river. "It sure is pretty here," my mother said. "I wonder if I could live in a place like this."

To Kevin her voice might have seemed admiring and wistful, but to me it sounded familiar, purposeful, as if she wanted something but wouldn't say what. As I looked out on the English-Philosophy building where I taught and took classes, and on the massive library where I'd spent so many hours, my mother's words connected in the shape of a loop that floated down over my head and tightened around my throat. Wait, I thought. Does she see this visit as a trial run for moving to Iowa?

Kevin said, "So you like it here?" and my mother said she did, very much, and then there was my thirteen-year-old self, muscling me aside with her anger and her attitude.

"What about the tornado that almost killed you?" I asked. "What about being scared to death in the basement and vowing you'd never come back?"

"Oh, that was awful," my mother replied, ignoring my tone and recounting her terror to Kevin, who remembered the day well. His car was still pockmarked from the hail.

"Anyway, I'm sure she wouldn't want me living here," my mother said, tossing her chin in my direction.

That was true. I'd often imagined taking care of my mother in her old age, tending to her needs and ailments the way she'd done for me in the first part of my life, but during the in-between years, the next ten or fifteen? It had taken a long time to assemble the life I now enjoyed, filled with writing and reading and friends who crafted the kind of stories and music and visual art that made my mother's nose wrinkle. My chest constricted at the thought of her moving into the middle of all that, suffocating me.

"Mom, with any luck *I* won't be living here in two years' time."

She frowned. "Oh, that's right. You'll be moving when you finally get a job. If you ever do get a job." She leaned toward Kevin and spoke out of the side of her mouth: "I'm starting to think she'll go right from college to collecting social security."

Kevin's face lit up. "Now there's an idea," he said, giving my shoulders a reassuring squeeze. "Grad school for the rest of our lives."

We walked back toward the center of town, past a marquee outside the Old Capital Mall that advertised, among other films, *William Shakespeare's "A Midsummer Night's Dream."* I'd chosen to teach the play precisely because the movie was coming out, but it hadn't gotten to Iowa in time. I wondered if it would still be here in two weeks.

Kevin's palm touched my back. "Look what's finally playing."

My mother followed our gaze and stopped walking. "You like that Shakespeare shit?" she asked, hands on her hips.

"Some of it," Kevin replied. "You don't?"

My mother shook her head, eyebrows furrowed and shoulders curving forward. "Nope. I don't know anything about it, and I don't want to."

I stole a glance at Kevin, wondering what he thought of this closing of the mind. Not only did my mother and I have different tastes but I had betrayed her by jumping class from the practical, dutiful, work-with-your-hands, save-your-money world she understood to a world of literature and art and ideas and travel to foreign countries, interests that formed what she thought of as an exclusionary club. Something like resentment shone on her face.

Kevin smiled at my mother. "I'll tell you what. Maybe one of these nights when you don't feel like going out, I'll take your daughter to that movie."

My mother's eyes widened, and the relief in her voice both pleased and pained me. "That sounds good! I go to bed early most nights anyway, so she's all yours."

The next morning, I lay on the twin futon in the living room, pretending to sleep. I'd heard my mother get up, use the bathroom, creep down the hallway to check on me and go back to bed, where she whispered to the cats and, I imagined, read from her Bible. It wasn't that I wanted to sleep more but that I wanted to remember and reflect.

Something had happened on our walk home the previous night. Between downtown and the corner where my mother and I bid Kevin goodnight, she began to tell stories about me, cocking her thumb in my direction and saying, "This one." "This one" always had her nose stuck in a book when she was little. "This one" used to dress herself in the most comfortable top and bottoms she owned, no matter if the patterns clashed. "Come to think of it, I'm not sure she's grown out of that," my mother said, glancing at the paisley leggings below my long blouse.

On the corner of College Street and Lucas Avenue, where we stopped to say goodbye to Kevin, my mother's comments intensified. "I'm sure she's told you what a pain I am to have around," she said.

In fact I hadn't told Kevin that, because it seemed too early in our relationship for family dirt. To keep him from having to respond, I said, "Mom, if I didn't want you to visit, I wouldn't have invited you."

Her eyes flashed as if she were winning at gin rummy or dominoes. "But you were ready to put me back on a plane to New York this morning before we even left the airport!" She turned to Kevin. "Can you imagine treating your mother that way?"

I raised both hands as if surrendering. "It's true. I did a horrible thing by paying the one-dollar parking fee at the airport, and she threatened to go back home."

At 5'6", my mother was a little taller than me, and as she stood rocking on her heels, enjoying this sparring session, I was struck again by her long, thin legs. Dancer's legs. Legs that once loved to polka. I remembered sitting on her bedroom floor as a child, watching her get dressed, feeling in love with those legs and everything else about her. She was beautiful, magical, powerful then.

"Can you imagine," she said, wearing what she would have described as a "shit-eating" grin. "I come all the way out here to visit her, and when I threaten to go back home again, she says, 'Suit yourself.' What do you think of that?" The game was for Kevin to side with her while winking at me, demonstrating his ability to carve a middle path between two difficult women.

Instead, Kevin smiled without crinkling his eyes, and said in a firm but gentle voice, "I think your daughter's gone out of her way to cook and clean and make sure your visit's a good one. You should appreciate that." His tone wasn't a rebuke so much as a quiet statement of fact, and it worked. My mother's teasing grin turned slowly into a nod, and we said goodnight and walked home in silence. Once we were in my apartment, her sandals tucked neatly beneath the bed, she sighed. "Well, that one might be a pretty good guy."

Becky and I had an evening ritual. Two or three times a week, around 6:00 or 7:00 p.m., one of us would call the other for a walk. We'd meet in the middle of the three-block distance between our apartments and stroll around

Iowa City's east side, past the stately homes along Sum-
mit Street, through the Longfellow neighborhood, to the
twin Moffitt houses—Hobbit-like cottages built in the
1920s from rounded stones. We walked and talked, pointing out small improvements to structures and yards, and
catching up on each other's lives.

Often we talked about family on these walks. Becky's
mother, in her seventies, still managed an independent
bookstore in Santa Barbara and regularly sent Becky
review copies of new books. Too many to keep up with,
Becky said once, and envy squeezed my throat. I couldn't
imagine having a parent with whom I could talk about
books or movies or politics.

I realized that was a lot to long for. The most accom-
plished graduate from Iowa's Nonfiction Writing Program
was Hope Edelman, whose best-selling book, *Motherless
Daughters*, had touched a cultural nerve by giving voice
to women whose mothers died relatively young. I was
grateful not to have suffered in that way and appreciated
that my mother still existed, that I could phone her and
visit with her and even be driven nuts by her. At the same
time, one of the defining characteristics of my life was the
loss of the mother who raised me into adolescence, even
though she hadn't literally died.

My graduate school years coincided with the era
of tell-all memoirs, when Mary Karr's *The Liar's Club*
recounted her mentally ill mother trying to stab her and
her sister with a knife, and Kathryn Harrison's *The Kiss*
detailed the consensual affair she began with her father
at age nineteen. In that time of "You think you've heard it
all? Listen to this!" I began to write quiet stories about my
mother. She wasn't aware of this, and I wonder now what
her reaction might have been if I'd shown her an essay

about that terrible-yet-wonderful time of her life when love was grand and the law so fucked up that a woman really could lose her kids, both of whom wanted to stay with her, because she loved another woman. I wonder if my mother would have felt mortified or liberated by the thought of my telling her story. Or maybe something in between.

Initially, though, she would have been infuriated, of that I'm sure. Which is why I didn't tell her. The little bit of writing I shared with her focused on travel, not on the secrets I'd implicitly agreed to keep as an adolescent. Now, as an adult, I no longer felt beholden to those secrets, but I didn't feel brave enough to come clean with my mother. I wanted to ease her burdens rather than intensify them, to make her happy despite knowing how impossible that was to do. When we walked through Iowa City together, I felt like a hypocrite, a fraud, a traitor, a coward. The only solace came from being all of these things because I was also a writer.

The next answering machine invitation came not from Kevin but from one of his housemates, Jane, letting me know that people were meeting up at the Airliner at 9:00 p.m. to watch an NBA playoff game. "Drop by if you're not doing anything," she said cheerily, and my mother insisted I go. "Enjoy your friends. I'm going to bed shortly, anyway."

I speed-walked into town. On the third evening of my mother's trip, I could honestly say things were going well, but there was relief in time away from her. Walking through College Green Park, my muscles relaxed and lungs emptied fully with each exhale.

Kevin smiled broadly when I slipped onto the barstool beside him. I hardly knew his housemates, a couple he'd once introduced me to on the street, but I thanked them for getting me out of the house. Mike poured me a beer as Jane said, "I made the call so your mother wouldn't think he was stealing you away from her."

Kevin wore an olive green baseball cap that made him look younger than thirty-three years. I liked the way he trimmed his thinning hair ultra-short, letting nature takes its course without subterfuge, and the way the hat made the freckles around his eyes stand out. His arms were freckled as well, the forearms appearing almost tan beneath light brown hair, and even his fingers, I noticed now, had some freckles on the backs. They were good hands, I thought as Kevin poured me a second beer and topped off the rest of the glasses. Sturdy yet soft, with straight, honest-seeming fingers. I imagined those fingers tracing my bare skin, pressing and exploring, and wondered what time I could reasonably return home that night. Any time I wanted, really, since I was an adult and my mother a solid sleeper. But then I thought about how uncomfortable it would be to leave Kevin's bed, pull on my jeans and tank top, walk the three blocks to my apartment and go to sleep alone on the narrow, lumpy futon in the living room.

As the evening wore on, Kevin and I moved imperceptibly closer to each other, thighs touching, radiating warmth through our clothes. The relationship was still too new for public displays, so we played it cool, enjoying the chaste proximity. Later on the walk home, Kevin split off from Mike and Jane to accompany me to my house, and we stood out front, in the shadow of the porch, and made out for a while, getting used to how our bodies interacted. Being forced into a slow start to our physical relationship was bizarre, but we agreed that the timing might be a good thing. "When can I see you again?" Kevin asked as we pulled apart, and I said I would call him the next day, would make up some excuse to get out of the house. "She likes you," I said.

Kevin nodded. "I feel like I know her already."

I asked him to explain, and he said she was like all those stubborn Irish ladies he'd grown up around, always complaining, always fretting about something, but also funny and kind. "You know what I'm talking about, right?"

I did not know what he was talking about. I'd been worried that Kevin would see similarities between my mother and me, recognizing in her a blueprint for my future. Instead, he viewed her through a lens that didn't really apply to me, and the relief of knowing that made my skin tingle. "Do you have any advice for dealing with a kind, funny, very stubborn Irish lady?" I asked, arms around his waist and face burrowing into his neck.

Kevin laughed and leaned back enough to look me in the eye. "You weren't kidding, she's a tough one. But you're smarter than she is, so you just have to cut her some slack."

Instantly, my cheeks flushed and defenses went into overdrive. My mother was very smart, I told him. *Very.* I was more educated, but she was perceptive, shrewd, someone whose intelligence he should not underestimate.

Kevin shook his head. "Come on. You know this, and there's nothing wrong with it. I'm not saying your mother isn't smart, but you've got the advantage. And that means you're more responsible for how things go between you."

I stood staring at him, the ground seeming to move beneath us. What did it mean to be more responsible than my mother for our relationship? And who did this guy think he was, pointing that out?

Kalona, Iowa. Population 2,300. First stop: the Amish grocery where lights and coolers are powered by kerosene, and where bags of pasta, rice, dried beans, chocolate chips, nuts, candy sell for a fraction of grocery store prices. An expression of happy nostalgia came over my mother's face as we walked the narrow aisles, the wood floor creaking under our feet. She had grown up in Wassaic, New York, a hamlet not far from the Connecticut border, where the single grocery store might have looked a lot like this in the 1940s, only with electricity and minus the white bonnet on the adolescent cashier.

Second stop: Kalona Historical Village, where we toured a complex of mid-nineteenth-century Mennonite homes and meeting halls. My mother admired the simple furniture and décor of the houses, imagining out loud what it would have been like to do the daily chores, washing clothes by hand and ironing them with a hunk of carved stone heated up in the fireplace. She was a life-long ironer. During my childhood she'd spent hours standing beside the dining room window each week, ironing every piece of wash she'd taken off the line—pants and shirts, of course, but also sheets and towels, handkerchiefs, even socks and underwear. My father and brother and I teased her about it, sometimes in a good-natured way and sometimes with frustration, when she was too busy ironing to play a board game or watch television with us. Even now, ironing was a Sisyphean task about which she didn't complain so much as give progress reports: the amount of time it had taken to finish, the number of items she'd handled. The first time I read Tillie Olsen's "I Stand Here Ironing," I laughed out loud at the daughter's comment, "Whistler painted his mother in a rocking chair. I'd have to paint mine standing over an ironing board." Only later did I think of my mother's obsessive ironing as a way of putting things right, smoothing the wrinkles, fashioning a narrative through-line for her life. If her clothes were clean and neat, she'd look respectable. Be respectable.

In Kalona Historic Village, we stepped into a replica kitchen, a homey space with a woodstove on top of which meals would have been cooked, and a sturdy, handmade table. My mother craned her neck toward cast iron cookware on a shelf and whispered, "We had those same pans when I was a kid."

"Like the pan you ate the soup out of?" I asked, and the wrinkles around my mother's pale blue eyes deepened with pleasure. "No, no, that was a little saucepan."

The soup incident took place on an evening when my grandmother was working late and my mother heated her own dinner. She was maybe ten years old, and instead of dirtying a bowl she'd later have to wash, she grabbed a spoon and ate her soup from the pan, sitting at the dining room window to spy on whoever might be walking through town. As it happened, a boy from her class was on his way home and the next day told everyone at school that my mother and grandmother were so poor they couldn't afford dishes. "And that was a lie," my mother said each time she told the story. "We had plenty of dishes."

As a child, I loved this story for its depiction of my mother as a lazy girl, more like me than like the ironer she became. Not until adulthood did I understand that the story stayed with her because of the truth in the other part of the boy's statement: they really were poor, so poor that some nights there wasn't even soup for dinner. So poor that, one summer, like the narrator in "I Stand Here Ironing," my grandmother arranged for her daughter to live elsewhere. But whereas Olsen's character stayed with relatives of her estranged father and came back skinny and disheveled, my mother thrived on a dairy farm in the country, where she lived with the family of one of her schoolmates. Each day she joined the other kids in chores that included milking cows, feeding chickens and sheep, tending an enormous vegetable garden. Her favorite part was mealtime, when the whole family sat down together, the parents at either end of the table, and in between the kids laughing and joking. My mother was born when her own mother was forty-five, the closest half-sibling sixteen, and her father was an inveterate bachelor who came around only when it suited him. She'd never had what she experienced on the farm: siblings around her age, two parents, a sense of abundance. Her skinny frame filled out that summer, her appetite driven by exercise and fresh air.

Then one day my grandmother arrived to take her home, and my mother's heart sank. She hid in the barn, sobbing and wishing she could stay on the farm for the rest of her life. "Can you imagine?" she said, eyes misting over as she told me this story for the first and only time. "My poor mother was so happy to come get me, and all I could do was cry."

It was mid-afternoon when we got back from Kalona, on such a pretty day it was a shame to be indoors. So I made iced tea and a plate of cheese and crackers while my mother set up dominoes on the porch. The weather was perfect, eighty degrees with no humidity, and we chatted as we played, saying hello to anyone who passed by.

Eventually, as we ate and drank and counted our dots, strategically laying out each domino, my mother began telling stories from the early years of her marriage to my father. Although she never talked about the breakup, she had a repertoire of narratives, many of which, like the soup pan story, illustrated a wrong done to her or an instance when she set someone straight. There was the time my parents argued on the way home from church and my mother got out of the car, slammed the door, and walked home as my father drove slowly along, begging her to get back in. There was the day I came home from the hospital, when my father dropped my mother and me off and then went to visit his own mother, leaving his wife to tend to the baby by herself. There were complaints about the disrespect my father showed her by dirtying a newly clean house or by leaving his wallet in his pants on a chair beside the bed as he slept, so that when my mother needed money for our school lunches, she had to sneak into his pockets like a thief.

That's the story she was rehearsing as I cast my eye across the table, looking for a way to make a two-one domino add up to a multiple of five.

"Why couldn't he have left the damn wallet on the dresser or the kitchen table? Or for that matter, why not just leave the lunch money out? Why was I the one who had to do everything for you kids?" Her voice was a cross between pleading and disgusted.

I'd heard these stories many times before, but the tone of my mother's voice today seemed especially bitter, her lips pursing as though the irritation were fresh. I wondered why she reached back for unpleasantness rather than soaking in the current day. Hadn't she enjoyed Kalona? Weren't we having a lovely time? There was nothing new in the story I'd heard dozens of times before, no attempt to look from a different angle or to understand her own agency; there was just the nursing of grudges that stained a beautiful May afternoon.

As my mother's eyes flitted between the dominoes already played and the ones standing on their sides before her, she moved on to a different grievance. Every night when my father got home from the plant, sometimes not until midnight or 1:00 a.m. if there'd been a problem with one of the machines, he'd walk into the house and call out, without even saying hello, "Make me a steak sandwich?" Sometimes she was sound asleep on the couch, his voice startling her upright.

I didn't dispute anything she said. I'd witnessed some of it and believed the rest, but now, sitting on my front porch beside a flowering lilac bush whose sweetness kept turning sour, new questions unfolded in my mind. Why hadn't my mother refused to make the sandwich? Why had she waited up, night after night, for her husband to get home from work even though she set her alarm for early in the morning to get the kids ready for school? Was the dynamic between my parents entirely my father's fault, or was it like the ironing, something my mother insisted on doing because it conformed to an idea of how a good woman should behave?

I knew better than to ask these questions aloud. She'd accuse me of siding with my father and disregarding her suffering, which wasn't true. I didn't side with my father, but I no longer sided with her. For all his faults, my father hadn't spoken ill of her to me in all the years since they'd separated, and she had done just the opposite. She had always wanted her kids to love her most, and only now, while living far away from her and thinking constantly about the stories we tell and how language works and the difference between what a sentence seems to say and what its author really means, did a revolutionary idea occur to me: I didn't have to listen. Just as my mother could have refused to make the steak sandwich, I could stop being her audience. If Kevin was right that I was the more responsible party in this relationship, then I had an obligation to change it.

I took a deep breath as she made her play, then picked up a domino and looked her in the eye. "Mom," I said gently, "I don't want to hear about this anymore."

Her forehead wrinkled. "What do you mean?"

"I don't want to hear your stories about Dad."

Her eyes widened before narrowing again. "You don't think I have a right to be mad about the way he treated me?" She sat up straighter, ready to argue her side.

"How you feel is how you feel," I said. "But he's my father, and I don't want you to talk about him like this to me. Sorry." My voice was steady and calm, although my hand trembled as I placed the domino on the table.

My mother turned silent after that, until the game was over and she'd won. Then she said, defiantly, "I kicked your butt," before getting up and walking down the steps to stand in the sun, hands on her hips, surveying the street as if trying to understand where in the hell her daughter had gone.

William Shakespeare's "A Midsummer Night's Dream" dramatizes the captivating strength of romantic attraction, the power plays and yearnings that accompany it, the invisible world responsible for turning reality upside down—all themes my mother would have appreciated if she could have ignored the bits of language she didn't understand, as everyone in the theater that night was doing, and let herself be carried along. Her sense of humor was very much in line with Shakespeare's, relishing comeuppance, applauding when people made jackasses of themselves for all the world to see.

The film was visually beautiful, the scenery lush and characters sexy, including Michelle Pfeiffer as the radiant Titania fawning over Kevin Kline's ass-headed Nick Bottom and Calista Flockhart's Helena, the poor woman in love with Demetrius who's in love with Hermia who's in love with Lysander, despite Hermia's father having betrothed her to Demetrius. Stanley Tucci's Puck was especially captivating, with his side-eye and half-smile before rushing off to drip love potion into a sleeping person's eye or, later, the antidote that returns everyone to normal. Watching the scenes felt like taking a vacation, like being carried far away and deposited back on an evening that sparkled.

Outside, Kevin and I walked along the pedestrian mall talking about the script, the casting, the makeup, the story, and by the time we reached the public library on Gilbert Street, we were holding hands. I hadn't noticed it happening and was surprised to discover our palms were joined, as if Shakespeare's magic had transformed us into a public couple.

We walked back to Kevin's house and carried bottles of beer outside to the porch swing. The porch was dark, in contrast to the streetlights and passing car headlights, and as we rocked, I leaned into Kevin's side, his arm around my shoulders, and looked at the small two-story house across the street. I'd lived on the second floor of that house during my first year in Iowa City, a year of trying to make new friends and become comfortable with myself as a doctoral student when all I really wanted to do was write. I felt misty-eyed thinking about the distance between that house and this porch. Now, at the beginning of a fellowship year, I sat swinging with a guy who increasingly seemed like a keeper and who expressed excitement at dating a writer. I appreciated that he'd ignored my instructions not to contact me for two weeks and that he'd orchestrated several little dates, all without making my mother feel like a fifth wheel.

His forehead touched my hair and I turned, finding his lips and settling into such quiet pleasure it was hard to stay seated. For a little while I was fully absorbed in the silent communication, the seeking and receiving, but soon I became aware of wanting to hurry, wrap things up, get away. I pulled back, tucking my head against Kevin's chest, and tried to identify the feelings. Had he done something to turn me off? Had I? No, it wasn't between us, it was something larger, something vaguely foreboding. I swatted at a moth flapping along my arm, and the emotion took on a recognizable shape: guilt. This much pleasure came accompanied by chagrin, and why was that? Because just three blocks away, straight down Burlington Street and one house in on Lucas, my mother slept in my bed, and I did not want to return to her.

Davenport for the riverboat casino, Dubuque for a drive along the Mississippi Bluffs. Lake MacBride up in Solon, lunch at Jonesy's Restaurant, known for pork patty sandwiches and deep-fried pickles. And around town, lots of walks and sitting on the front porch and talking about what would come next in my mother's life. I suggested volunteering, taking a class of some sort, learning a language, but nothing appealed to her. "The days are so long," she moaned. "I don't know what I'll *do*."

As my mother's visit drew to a close, she became more and more worried about the future. She dreaded going home, couldn't imagine filling the empty space where a job used to be. I had the sense that if I asked her to stay for two more months, she would accept with relief.

On our last full day together, we had breakfast on the porch, went for a walk, then returned to my apartment with no plans. My mother disappeared into my bedroom, and a few minutes later I found her stretched out on the bed, four pillows propped under her back. "The time here has really flown by," she said, scratching the head of the calico cat, who was always happy to lounge in bed with a human.

Seeing my mother there, gray hair against my pillow, belly stretching her blouse and those long legs emerging from her shorts and reaching diagonally toward the foot of the bed, I felt a tsunami of tenderness. I had known this woman, this body, my entire life. I had loved her my entire life, first with the unencumbered adoration of a toddler, later with the capacious devotion of a child who recognizes flaws and feels more deeply because of them, and later still with emotion so steeped in sorrow and distrust that it turned inside-out, resembling impatience and judgment. But I did love her, as steadfastly as I would ever love anyone, I thought then, standing in my bedroom with the desire to help her flooding my throat.

What could I do? In the last few days she'd been talking about moving to Las Vegas to escape the New York winters, and the more she talked, the more serious this possibility seemed. I thought it was a terrible idea, partly because she knew no one there besides my brother and would have to start over from scratch. But more importantly, I had seen how she played slots at the riverboat casino, going into a kind of trance as she fed twenty-dollar bills into the machines. A woman who gambled like that should not live in Vegas.

But my mother was as stubborn as Kevin said, and I knew there was no countering whatever she set her mind to. Well, I thought, if I couldn't help with the future, I could at least focus on the present. If I couldn't quiet her mind, I'd tend to her body. "How about a foot massage?"

A pinched expression took over my mother's face. "You want to rub my feet?"

"Sure," I said, before retrieving a bottle of peppermint foot lotion from the bathroom and a throw pillow from the couch. I knelt at the foot of the low bed and placed the throw pillow under my mother's left calf. "Are you comfortable?"

She wiggled her shoulders, burrowing into the pillows beneath her back. "Why do you want to rub my feet?"

I thought of the various lovers who had rubbed my feet, and I theirs, and also of my friend Doug, who had once offered an exquisite foot massage on his living room floor, a kindness that was intimate but not sexual or romantic. I wondered if anyone in my mother's life had ever rubbed her feet without being paid for it.

I swallowed hard and took a deep breath, warming the lotion between my hands before stroking the top of her foot. "Because it'll feel good," I said, trying to imitate the calming way massage therapists speak.

My mother's eyebrows remained wrinkled as she looked at me, but I focused on her foot, holding its heel while working a thumb into the arch, and eventually her eyes closed.

For someone who had worked standing for most of her adult life, my mother's feet were surprisingly smooth. I rubbed and kneaded, first one foot and then the other, paying attention to the ankles and lower calves as well. By the time I'd finished, my mother seemed tranquil, almost sleepy. "You could do that for a living," she whispered, and I said that was good to know, in case the whole teaching career didn't pan out.

"Now let me rub your feet," she added, the lethargy in her voice belying her ability to do any such thing.

I said no thanks, and she huffed a little about how I must not think she could do a good job. "I ought to pay you, then," she said, starting to sit up. "The way you paid for my massage last week."

"You know what would be a great payment, Mom? Just saying thanks."

She lay back against the pillows. "Well, thank you then," she said, tone cranky but the expression on her face content.

That evening, after my mother fell asleep, I walked over to Kevin's house for half an hour in his bedroom. He sat in a desk chair while I straddled his lap, my thighs stretching almost to the point of pain, and we enjoyed the last of this kind of interaction, desire building with no outlet. My mother's flight was at 2:00 the next afternoon, and Kevin and I planned to fall into bed as soon as I returned from the airport—his bed, my bed, what difference did it make? We'd cross the line into consummated romance, and afterwards we'd order Chinese food or pizza or walk to the Indian restaurant just off the ped mall, muscles still humming, and later we'd fall into bed again, as often as we liked in the weeks and months to come.

Back at home, I curled onto the futon in my living room, feeling excited and happy. My mother had had a good trip. I'd fed her well, calmed her down as much as possible, kept my impatience mostly in check. And the next day, I would take her to the airport, content to have done all I could for her.

But during that night, something went awry, as if Puck had stolen in through the window and dripped potion into my eye. My dreams offered heavy, nonsensical scenes that rippled with sorrow and woke me several times, head aching and stomach churning. When I opened my eyes in the morning to a beam of sunlight covering most of the living room floor and the sound of the shower running, the physical pain was gone but tears streamed down my cheeks, wetting the pillowcase.

I got up and washed my face in the kitchen sink, then went to the bedroom to get dressed. My mother was already packed, the bed neatly made and her sneakers sitting in a clear plastic bag atop her suitcase. Looking at her things arranged for travel made sadness expand in my chest until all the colors of the day melted in streaks.

We spent the morning in the restless state that often precedes travel. Or at least I did. When I asked about the short layover in Chicago's O'Hare Airport, where gates can be a long distance from one another, my mother shrugged. "I'll manage." She was considerably more subdued than she'd been during her stay.

Perhaps because of her resignation, my sadness turned into the kind of heartache that makes it difficult to talk. Or breathe. I kept thinking that my mother wouldn't get home before 8 p.m. at the earliest, which was 9 p.m. in New York, and that danger lurked in the two flights and in the car she'd left at the airport and in her second-floor apartment with its front and back staircases—what if someone had broken in while she was gone? I felt jittery and nauseous thinking of her going home alone.

At the same time, impatience rumbled beneath the sadness. When my mother wanted to leave early for the airport "just in case," I asked with irritation: "In case of what?" When she insisted on picking up her own carry-on bag, I snapped, "You're out of work because of a bad back!" When she nudged me in the airport's check-in line and raised her eyebrows at a young woman's facial piercings, I shook my head the way adults do with misbehaving children. All the while, my stomach tightened further. Here was my mother, my first love, the woman at the center of my child's world and at the edges as well, the person I still thought of whenever there was news, good or bad, whenever a snowstorm struck the east coast, whenever I woke in the middle of the night and couldn't get back to sleep, feeling around the edges of my mind for what might be wrong. Please, I often thought, offering an atheist's prayer to no one, let my mother be safe and happy.

Outside security, we hugged goodbye. I wanted to tell her I loved her, but it was all I could do to say, "Call me when you get home," without turning into a sniveling mess. So I stood back and watched as she fed her carry-on into the x-ray machine, emerged on the other side of screening, and stepped onto the escalator. Almost immediately she turned around, searching for me among the couple dozen people outside security. I stretched my arm up, waving, but her gaze scanned over my head and she turned back around, having concluded far too readily that I'd left. This was just before everyone carried cell phones, before I had a way of telling her that I was there, of course I was there, right where she expected me to be. "I would never abandon you!" I wanted to shout, and the tears were coming now, streaming down my face and rolling into my mouth.

The tears continued as I walked outside, got into the car, and turned onto the interstate. I expected the emotion to subside with distance, but it escalated until I was wailing like a child, mouth open and eyes squeezed to slits, gasping for breath. When those spasms subsided, deep keening sobs took over, sobs that wouldn't stop, not on the drive home and not in my living room, where I curled onto the couch and pressed my face into a pillow, the emotion so strong and physical and unexpected that I had no ability to curb it. *My mother is gone,* I kept thinking, with a sadness bigger than that day and bigger than the first time she left me. It was as if she'd died, or worse, as if I were the mother and she were the daughter and I'd lost her.

An hour passed. Then two. Kevin was surely wondering what happened, why I hadn't gone straight to his house. I kept washing my face, drinking water, admonishing myself to get it together, but then I'd be back on the couch, crying and gasping, unable to speak. Years later, the first time I saw my mother's body in a casket the day before we buried her in the Las Vegas desert, I would cry in a similar way, recognizing the grief that had begun in Iowa City.

At 5:30 p.m., the phone rang. I blew my nose, took a sip of water, listened as Kevin's voice played through the answering machine's speaker. "Just calling to make sure you're OK," he said with a tone of concern, and I picked up the receiver.

"Hi," I squeaked before the tears began again. I managed to say that I was fine, just sad, that my mother's leaving had triggered something I didn't understand.

Kevin offered to let me relax that evening and said he'd call again the next day, but I didn't want to be alone with this crazy grief. By then I'd been crying for four hours, with no end in sight and no explanation I could articulate. All I knew was that my mother had come for two weeks, the longest amount of time we'd spent together since I was a child, and even though I hadn't wanted her to stay longer, I missed her.

Kevin walked over and held me as I continued to cry, and eventually I pulled myself together enough to walk into town. We sat at the bar of a restaurant that was otherwise full, our seats up against one another, Kevin rubbing my back as we ate and I continued to weep. It was bizarre and painful and sweet, and already I knew I'd sleep alone that night. Whatever this breakdown was, it needed to finish before I could turn my full attention to the next love of my life.

On the walk home, I sniffled and said, by way of apology, "Even though she's not here anymore, my mother's still getting in our way." Kevin laughed and squeezed my hand. We talked about how much fun dating had been these last two weeks and how much more fun the next weeks were bound to be. It was summer. We were both done with grading. He had finished his comprehensive exams, and I had nothing to do next year but write. We could spend all the time we wanted together.

But first, a test: I asked Kevin to tell me what he thought of my mother, what he *really* thought. He tipped his head back and laughed in a full-throated way, and I waited, holding my breath because however much I might agree with his impressions, I would turn against him in a heartbeat if his assessment were too harsh. My mother. My poor, beloved mother.

Kevin let go of my hand and reached around my shoulders to pull me close and navigate the trap I'd set. "She's a real character," he said. "She means well and can be hilarious, but . . ." He paused to laugh again before squeezing me tighter and saying the words I'd waited my whole life to hear, even though they scraped my heart raw: "It's hard to believe you're her daughter."

BACKSTITCH

On the bus from LaGuardia Airport to Grand Central Station I'm thinking about the night, thirty years ago, with the boy who lived in Hell's Kitchen. On 57th street, in an apartment on the 57th floor, with a view of the Empire State Building.

He was Cuban, this boy, with bright blue eyes, and his parents were away for the weekend, visiting relatives in Miami. I had no idea then what it all meant, the cramped apartment, the way he spat the name "Fidel," the sense of loss that hung over the family. His mother was a secretary at the neighborhood Catholic church, his father a tailor.

That night in the apartment it was the blue-eyed boy, his two older brothers, and me, a seventeen-year-old girl come down on the train from Poughkeepsie. For dinner we ate homemade eggrolls, all four of us crowded onto a wrought iron balcony in the midtown sky. Later the brothers went out dancing and the boy and I went to bed, where we tried once again to close the gap between desire and what his body was willing to do, and in the middle of the night, maybe 2 a.m., one of the brothers came home with a couple of friends and a girl who was drunk. The blue-eyed boy and I got out of bed and said hello, and the brother announced that this girl had split the crotch of her pants on the dance floor. She was blonde, I remember, and smiled in a silly way, as if she didn't quite know who she was.

"What are we supposed to do about it?" my boy said, not unkindly.

The brother glanced at me. "I thought somebody might be able to sew them for her."

As it happened, I knew how to sew. Not well, but enough to keep a pair of pants together for a night. And of course there was plenty of thread in the home of a tailor.

Our pants were all too tight then, so I wasn't surprised to discover, when the girl came out of the bathroom wrapped in a towel and handed me her jeans, that the place where they'd split was wet and yeasty. The seam kept slipping from my fingers as I sewed, and as everyone talked and laughed around me, I began to feel like the workhorse version of Cinderella preparing her step-sister for the ball. But I wanted the boy to appreciate how willing I was to pitch in, to adore me even, so I didn't complain. After the girl was dressed again and the kitchen had emptied out, he pulled me onto his lap and kissed my neck. "You have many talents," he said.

The next day he borrowed a friend's car and drove me to Grand Central Station, which I now know would have been a fine walk, and that was the last I saw of him. We talked on the phone a few times, and months later he called to let me know, in a roundabout way, that he had taken up with the friend whose car he had borrowed, a guy so handsome and sweet I'd have taken up with him myself if given the chance.

All these years later it's hard to remember how it felt to be in love with the blue-eyed boy, but I remember very clearly that girl's jeans, turned inside out, seam against seam as I sewed through the moist denim until it wouldn't come apart again. This is not the sort of detail you share, not with the guy, not with the friend who picked you up at the Poughkeepsie train station and asked for every detail of your weekend in the city. But it's the kind of detail that becomes permanent, bubbling up sometimes when you least expect it: the moisture, the needle, the sense that desire is everywhere, all the time, the seam between past and present porous. She would be in her fifties now, that girl, still older than me.

MY SKY, MY LIFE

In mid-October, pale yellow leaves skittered along East 40th Street, dodging the tiny, whirring wheels of my suitcase. On the corner of Fifth Avenue, the morning breeze carried the sweet glaze of hairspray, the sharp burn of a pretzel cart, aromas that intensified the gorgeous day. I, too, felt intensified, hyper-aware and eager to arrive, despite the anxious clenching in the center of my chest.

As I approached the hotel on West 40th Street, a besuited man opened the lobby door, looking at something beyond my shoulder. Just last month this block had been filled with runway models from New York's Fashion Week, sashaying in and around Bryant Park. What must it be like, I wondered, to enter a sleek lobby, all elbows and hip bones and sharp attitude, as if you belonged here? Or maybe the models, too, felt out of place, self-conscious and trying to pass. I lowered my shoulders, raised my rib cage, released the flesh of my lips from between my teeth. Confidence, after all, is a state of mind.

A desk clerk with perfect makeup and a Caribbean lilt to her voice typed my name into a computer and skimmed the reservation, after which her large eyes met mine for a couple seconds too long. Her smile contained what looked like a question, and I imagined her wondering why on earth the plain-looking woman before her, a woman without a platinum credit card or corporate discount, was paying $650 for a single night's hotel stay. Her eyes glanced at the screen again before flitting up and landing once more on a woman in need of a manicure, without a designer handbag or French perfume, and without an attitude either, I hoped she noticed, even though it wasn't quite true. I did have an attitude about this sort of place and the people who can afford it, people who waste and demand and need more than everyone else to make them feel valid. I wanted to tell the desk clerk I wasn't one of them, wasn't like the other people who stayed here. But what did that mean?

In the elevator, I thought about what $650 had purchased at other times in my life. In college I'd paid that amount for a rusting, dangerously fast Camaro that I drove until rain dripped into my lap. Later I paid that same amount for a round-trip ticket to Spain with an airline known for arriving, in typical Spanish fashion, late. $650 was the monthly rent on the first apartment Kevin and I shared during graduate school, and the cost, tax and delivery included, of a new dishwasher for our condo in Chicago. Each of those purchases constituted a decent deal. But this week all I had to show for my money was a reservation for the second-cheapest hotel room in Midtown. The first-cheapest, at $275, was a long walk from public transportation and had so many negative reviews online that it had seemed perversely reasonable to upgrade.

Upon entering the room, I realized I didn't know where the dividing line lay between budget and luxury in Manhattan—four hundred dollars? five hundred?—but I'd leapt over it. The spaciousness, sleek blonde furniture, and wall of windows made me stop and ask aloud, "Who do I think I am?"

I'd been asking that question a lot lately. A few weeks before, I'd turned forty-three, which meant I was no longer in the vestibule of middle age. I was over the threshold now, into the great room, with its dust motes floating in the sun, its overstuffed chairs beckoning. Forty-three is the age when one finally has to concede some things, and that had been fine with me until the biggest thing I had to concede turned out not to be so.

Two months before, for the first time in my life, a pregnancy test had turned positive. Immediately, vibrantly positive. When Kevin walked in a few minutes later and asked what was wrong, I said, "It looks like I'm pregnant, if you can believe that." My tone sounded like my own mother's when she thought something was bullshit, and this surprised me almost as much as the test result. Only later did I realize that the happy surprise of being pregnant was laced, from the first moment, with potential loss. After delaying the decision to start a family for so long, focusing on education and career and ignoring reports about infertility over thirty-five, I'd tossed aside birth control as if audacity alone might defeat the odds. Once it had, I immediately wondered if the good fortune could last.

I still wondered. "The fetus," we called it, knowing that babyhood was a long way off and without guarantee. Kevin and I had agreed not to tell anyone about the pregnancy before the twelve-week genetic testing, and I couldn't shake the notion that one wrong move on my part could lead to karmic miscarriage. A $650-hotel-room, for example, might scream "hubris" to the fertility gods even though, in the end, I wouldn't be the one paying for it.

I was in New York to promote my first published book, which I would read from later that night. It was a small gig, no expenses paid, and I'd planned to write the travel costs off my taxes, but after I booked the room, the price gnawed at me until I got up the courage to walk down the hall to the office of my department chair and ask if the university might reimburse this trip. A reading in a curated series was sort of like a conference presentation, wasn't it? Especially since I wouldn't be requesting any other travel money this year? The chair had blinked for about three seconds before shrugging cheerfully. "I don't see why not."

So I really had no cause to complain, here in a room that was bigger than most Manhattan studios, but I couldn't shake the feeling that I was doing something wrong, reaching beyond my practical roots, courting comeuppance. If I weren't pregnant, if I hadn't taught until 9:30 the previous night and gotten up at 6:00 this morning to head to the airport, I'd have skipped the hotel altogether and, after the reading, would have ridden the train ninety miles north to my father's house in Poughkeepsie. That's what the normal version of me would have done, and it still seemed vaguely sensible. I shook my head at the Scandinavian furniture, the perfect whiteness of the bed. The bathroom was large enough to pace in, the tub shockingly deep. I opened the complimentary bottle of bath salts and inhaled its earthy scent, harrumphing.

Then I phoned my friend James, who lives in Queens, and agreed to meet him in the lobby in ninety minutes. After stripping to my underwear, I slid between the sheets, the thread count for which was advertised in a brochure on the nightstand. *Ridiculous*, I thought, as the feather duvet settled around my shoulders, ushering in such a deep sleep that when the alarm clock chimed an hour later, I woke confused. Where, I wondered, was this earthly paradise?

As always, James smelled both sweet and spicy, like a meal I wanted to devour. His orange sweater caressed my cheek until he finally let go and stepped back to give me the once over. "You look sexy," he said, drawing out the last word in his gorgeous Colombian accent. He looked sexy, too, with his spiky black hair and close-trimmed beard and the always-serious expression that softened easily into a smile or a laugh.

The last time I was in New York, I stayed with James and his partner, Jose, sleeping on a comfortable sofa in their living room. Now, a European friend of Jose's was holed up with them for a month, so there wasn't space for me. I didn't want James to feel bad about that, but the price of the hotel room weighed so heavily I couldn't help myself. We were barely out of the lobby before the cost flew from my lips, followed quickly by the explanation of the university reimbursement. That part mattered as lit-tle to James as it did to me—the point was that so much money for a single night was absurd. "Oh my God!" James gasped, stopping with a hand to his heart. He glanced back toward the hotel with a look of disgust, his black eyebrows furrowed. "I totally would have kicked that German girl out if I'd known."

James was one of my favorite people in the world. As we crossed avenues and then streets, he attended to me, placing his hand on my back as we passed a group of young men, guiding me ahead of him with the gentlest touch. There was care in his voice as he leaned in to say, "How is your mother doing?" and in the way he called me "cariño," which reminded me of living in Spain years before, where friends addressed one another with casual terms of endearment—my love, my beauty, my heart. Kevin and I had agreed not to tell anyone about the pregnancy until after the results of genetic testing the next month, but as James and I walked, I realized that if something were to go wrong, James would say exactly the right thing. When Kevin and I agreed not to tell anyone, we meant family. James, I thought as his hand clasped mine, didn't count.

But James had counted, not so long before. How to say it without sounding cliché? We met three years before at an artist colony in the Berkshires, where we'd each been invited to spend a month free of charge, living and writing in a converted barn on the former estate of the poet Edna St. Vincent Millay. The setting was lush and fragrant and the view outside my studio window so green that for the first few days I walked around in a state of astonishment because someone thought I deserved this, an entire month in a beautiful place. All I had to do was whatever I felt like: write and read and take walks and eat dinner each night with the other residents, one of whom was James.

There were six of us in all, three writers and a painter in the barn, and up the hill in the main house, a photographer and a sculptor. We came and went at our own times, spending the day working and hiking and napping and talking on our cell phones out in the middle of the dirt road, where reception was best. Only at dinnertime did we all come together, and the highlight of each day, the reward for plugging away hour after hour on an essay that wasn't coming together yet, was the moment when I walked up the hill, entered the main house, and approached the table. James was often there already, nodding intently at another resident, his serious expression cracking into a bright smile when he saw me. Over dinner we talked and joked, dominating the conversation, agreeing on every political topic that came up and waxing sarcastic about the war in Iraq, the upcoming presidential election, the pope, scientology. Later we'd walk back to the barn, the evening air thick with country smells, and share a glass of Scotch in the hallway before going back to work. Before long, I was in love with him.

I don't mean that I loved him. Love needs time, much longer than a month, to take root and grow. But being *in love,* that early, dangerous stage of mild obsession, can happen quickly and intensely, without one's consent or control.

Kevin and I fell in love during the summer, when we had an abundance of time together. Mornings, as I ate breakfast on my front porch, he'd walk down the street, bookbag over his shoulder, smiling broadly. He was on his way to the library or the coffee shop, somewhere quiet to read and think, but first he wanted to say hello. Sometimes he stopped for a quick chat, rubbing my back and chatting before walking off again, and sometimes we fell into bed for an hour before resuming our separate days. So much of the pleasure of that time came from the growing rhythm, how we collided and spun away, discovering each time we intersected again that we liked each other more.

During those early months I had a recurring dream that one or both of us was married, or seriously involved with someone else, that our love affair was laced with regret. Some mornings I woke to find Kevin lying face-down beside me, my enormous orange cat atop his back, and the relief of our situation made me giddy. There was no guilt, no sadness, just all the possibility in the world and a welling up of gratitude for how open and available we both were.

By the time I went to the Millay Colony five years later, Kevin and I had settled into a comfortable life. We lived a short walk from Lake Michigan, rode the El to our teaching jobs, visited the east coast a couple times each year. Before my residency we'd spent a few days at his mother's house in Massachusetts, and when we said goodbye at a rest area on the turnpike, him headed back to Chicago and me into the Berkshires, I missed him so much my chest ached. Every day I looked forward to arriving home at the end of the month, to sharing a bed and a breakfast table and going out to dinner and to the movies and talking and talking the way we always did.

In the meantime, I talked with James. We learned about each other in short spurts, and the daily rhythm of offering bits of story, separating and then coming together again, was as seductive as the early time with Kevin. So much of romance involves seeing yourself reflected back in the expression of someone who enjoys you, and James has the kind of face that shows, and mirrors, appreciation.

In the barn, I developed the habit of rising early and going immediately upstairs to my studio. After a few hours of work, I would stand up, stumble to the couch, and fall into a deep sleep. The sounds of the other artists—the painter washing out brushes in the common sink and the poet down the hall closing her studio door when she came in from a walk—seeped into my dreams, into scenes that turned bacchanalian, filled with raucous crowds and music and dancing and wild flirtations that led to even wilder dalliances. The dreams were like the flip side of life in Italo Calvino's short-short story "Chloe," where everyone goes about their individual business in perfect chastity, nodding heads as they pass on the street without becoming entangled. Such a world, Calvino writes, trembles with "voluptuous vibration."

That's how that month in the Berkshires felt, voluptuous and also furtive, especially once James started appearing in my dreams, attending to me, courting me, sidling up and pressing his lips into my hair, speaking into my ear, and the next moment pressing his body into mine in the way that dream-sex works, part theory, part metaphor, part animalistic drilling. I would wake sweaty and pulsing, all the energy of the day's creative work funneled into a nerve pathway so stimulated that the studio, the barn, the entire estate of Edna St. Vincent Millay became subsumed into it, as if I were turning inside out and encompassing the mountainside.

Footsteps on the stairs, someone just outside the door, and I lay very still, breath held, waiting for a knock that never came because the cardinal rule at an artist colony is: don't interrupt the creative process. But was this the creative process? It certainly felt that way, as though the crescendo, the release, the pyrotechnic explosion of synapses firing all at once and then rolling away like a spent thunderstorm, seemed essential to the next session's work, to being able to go downstairs to the bathroom, pour a glass of water (James's door all the while closed), and return to my desk, where I'd sometimes lose track of time and have to run up the hill to dinner.

On Third Avenue, we walked slower. The sun was so lovely that we edged toward the street, away from the buildings' shadows, turning our faces up as we talked about the sales figures on James's novel, which had come out a few months before and was already being translated into five languages. There would be more languages eventually, and international prizes and a movie, but for now we talked about the relief of having books out in the world and about the new projects we were starting and about some people we both knew in New York. The whole time I felt divided in two.

On the one hand I listened, asked questions, engaged in the conversation; on the other I floated, conscious of the blood expanding my veins. My body didn't look pregnant, not from any angle, and for the most part I didn't feel it, either. There'd been no morning sickness or fatigue. The only physical change so far was a slight bloating of my midsection and a corresponding fullness in my breasts. I wore gauzy black pants from a maternity store, with a wide waistband that folded over and that later, if there were a later, would extend up over my belly. On top was a tunic that clung to my chest before draping around my middle, making me feel, as I walked down the street linking arms with James, surprisingly sexy.

We sat at a wrought-iron table on the sidewalk, in metal chairs that curved back just enough for my stomach to feel on display. We each ordered a cup of tea and a slice of cake, and I kept shifting, leaning back with one leg crossed and hands clasped to hide my mid-section, then sitting up close to the table, feet flat on the ground, sipping. Back and forth, trying to get comfortable, trying to figure out when and how to say the words and how to *be* afterwards, once the words made the situation real.

At Millay Colony, James and I had snuck away a few times, taking my car down the mountain into town or up over the mountain and across the Massachusetts state line. We went to bars where we drank whiskey and talked about our lives, about his upbringing in Colombia, with a mother who had been his father's long-time mistress until he left his wife and married her, a mother both tremendously strong and maddeningly passive. James's novel centered on an entire town of women like that, women with no idea of their own power until a group of guerrilla revolutionaries forces all the town's men to join their ranks, leaving the women to fend entirely for themselves. Over the next years, the women slowly adapt to the absence of men, and the community that arises looks very much like the socialist utopia men have always fought for but never attained. The women pair up in exquisite love affairs, devise a new way of marking time based on monthly cycles, lose the need for clothing and most material goods. They become edenic creatures, satisfied by one another, their need for men evaporating.

How I loved sitting on a barstool listening to James choose his words to perfection and pronounce them in a way that was subtle and glowing, as if they were wrapped in beautiful paper. He told me about the novel, which was as feminist a story as any I'd heard, and about his job waiting tables and about how he'd come to the U.S. at twenty-six, leaving an advertising career in Bogotá and working menial jobs in New York while learning English. Within a few years he was accepted into the MFA program at Columbia University, which he still seemed to regard as a surprising turn of events.

I told James about my book, a travel memoir focused on Spain, and about my family, how my mother left my father in the mid-1970s, when lesbianism was a secret so dark it took more than a decade, until my mid-20s, for me to share the story with anyone. I told him about Kevin, who had happily moved to Chicago when I got a job and who remained as content to live in sin as I was. James was impressed that we weren't married and didn't plan to be, and I liked that he was impressed. I wanted to impress him every day, to dress nicer and write better and be cooler so that the smile he cast on me across the dinner table wouldn't fade.

One night we came back early from a bar in town where everyone from the colony had gathered. A new moon had made the drive especially dark, and emerging from my car, we saw the Milky Way spread across the sky, diamonds affixed to a newly erased chalkboard. "Here," James said, jogging to the barn and reaching inside to snap off the floodlight, after which the world, the earth, felt so precarious it seemed we might slip off its surface and take our floating place among the stars. There is nothing so humbling as a pitch-black night with a galaxy unfurled across it. The sheer number of stars puts to rest any existential thoughts because standing in our tiny world, hurtling through a universe filled with stars and planets and maybe even civilizations, what's the point of wondering about anything? What chance is there of arriving at even a glimmer of truth, given the sheer volume of perspectives possible in all that space?

I went to bed that night feeling satisfied. There was nowhere else I wanted to be, nothing else I craved. In two weeks I would return to my happy life with Kevin, and in the meantime, there was only writing and napping and walking and feeling the marvelous gift that was this burgeoning friendship with James.

The next afternoon, I lay on my studio couch, heart racing and pelvis throbbing, after a dream in which James and I were entwined in my parents' bed, the double-bed of my childhood, and he was lying on his side behind me, clutching me so tight it almost hurt except that it didn't hurt, and when my eyes opened I had no clue where I was. A desire to leave this place forced me up and out to the car, then down the mountain to a café where I drank coffee and stared at a newspaper, wondering what it meant to feel an attraction so strong it veered toward repulsion. When I was with James, when we shared a meal or traded stories, I felt calm, relaxed, not the least bit flustered. But as soon as we parted, his presence grew in my mind until I had trouble sitting still.

What did it all mean, especially since a real affair held no allure? I didn't find myself wishing James weren't gay or imagining what things might be like if he were attracted to me. I didn't want to be involved with James. I told myself he was simply a safe object for my emotions, that our compressed living situation created a false intimacy and his sexual orientation allowed for the emotional pleasure of an affair without any of the messiness. But as the residency progressed, I fell into the mild psychosis that often comes with secret love. Some days I grew irritable, anxious, and confused, as if I'd transformed into outrageous Sally Bowles, pining for dear, queer Christopher Isherwood.

One night James and I exchanged some of our published work, and when we saw each other the next afternoon, each eager to talk about what we admired, I felt the kind of heady relief that comes from confessing one's feelings. It was a beautiful July day, dragonflies riding each other across the field in front of the barn, and butterflies dancing their drunken way from flower to flower. James and I met on the path to the main house, him going there and me coming back, and when we gushed about what we'd read, each relieved to have liked the other's work so much, it felt like we were making a blood pact. Later James gave me a CD he'd burned of a Portuguese woman singing *fado* in a voice cracked with pain and passion. "I love dramatic music," he said while holding his palm to his heart, eyebrows scrunched, pronouncing the word "love" like "loaf," which I loved.

That night over dinner James told a funny story about a platonic roommate he'd once kicked out after realizing the guy used James's moisturizer every day. "What kind of moisturizer was it?" I asked in a gently mocking tone, and James met me right there, hand on heart, eyebrows scrunched again. "Lancôme," he said, caressing the syllables and holding a deadly serious expression while shaking his head almost imperceptibly, encouraging me to laugh. That's what I fell in love with: James's ability to be and to think about being in the exact same moment. As if there were two versions of him, each present at the same time, the pair of them wry and handsome, critical and empathetic, attentive and flirtatious and utterly addictive.

At the sidewalk café, we sat on adjacent sides of the table, savoring each bite of cake and the beautiful weather and the people walking past, dressed in everything from short-shorts to jeans and leather jackets. We talked about Kevin and Jose and about the minutiae of life until it began to feel duplicitous not to utter the words bouncing around in my brain. I wanted to say them, but I felt wary of how they'd transform my identity from that of a writer, traveler, college professor, roles I'd dreamed of inhabiting for a good part of my life, into the most ordinary role of all: mother. I felt almost embarrassed by the stereotypical turn life was taking.

My hands shook and I nearly started to giggle, the way I would have done three years before if I'd decided to tell James I'd fallen in love with him. The nervousness I felt now had a lot in common with infatuation, which is all about possibility, all about a future that sparkles, transforming from black-and-white into Technicolor even when that future is only a vague impression. When I fell in love with Kevin, I took the long view, thinking about the possibility of living together, belonging to one another, becoming something like a family. When I fell in love with James, the view was altogether different. Maybe what I wanted back then was exactly what I had right now: the security of knowing I would see him again and again, that we would continue to orbit each other closely for years to come.

"So, I do have another bit of news that I haven't really told anyone yet," I said, setting my fork down and looking into James's eyes.

His lips turned down, eyebrows furrowed. "What is it?" he asked, body tensed as if bracing for a diagnosis. My voice had once again betrayed my emotions, sounding more serious than I'd intended.

"Don't worry, it's not bad news," I said, and as James's face relaxed I remembered my first swimming lesson at eight years old, in Pulaski Pool, where the college-aged instructors ran us through a series of drills aimed at getting our faces into the water before we lined up at the deep end and, one by one, jumped off the diving board into a depth of twelve feet. I couldn't swim, couldn't even exhale with my face in the water; during the drills I'd simply held my breath and waited for water to seep into my sinuses. I remembered walking down the diving board and looking at the deep end, where a young woman treading water promised to catch me as soon as I went under, and thinking that this might be the end of my life but that if it wasn't, if I managed to survive the fall and the impact and the journey to the ladder at the side of the pool, I would be a different person. I remembered how hard it was to step forward off the board and how, once I'd committed, there was no way to undo that step.

When the words "I'm pregnant," reached his ears, James's eyebrows shot up and his face broke into a dramatic, emotional smile, the kind of smile that validates its recipient to the core. He rocked forward into my arms, laughing and saying congratulations and kissing my hair. "How amazing!" he kept saying. "Wow!" His eyes dropped down over my chest and abdomen and back again, until I felt like an exquisite corpse, something beautiful and grotesque, something whose parts both do and don't go together. I thought once again of the expensive hotel room, of the ease with which I'd booked it, hardly recognizing myself. Who did I think I was?

"You understand that I'm forty-three," I said.

James waved as if swatting a fly. "So what?"

"So, the doctor was pretty surprised." I told him the whole story, how we'd quit using birth control three years before and how we were lazy about watching the calendar and how when the OB/GYN asked if this were a spontaneous pregnancy, I had no idea what she meant, so I joked that we'd been together for almost nine years, how spontaneous did she expect us to be? James laughed and marveled and then turned serious when I told him the statistics on miscarriage at this age. That was all I expected to say, since why dwell on the good or the bad when what will happen will happen regardless of what we do to encourage it, no matter what kind of hotel we spend the night in. But James is a man who feels things deeply, and the expression on his face was so intense I couldn't stop there.

The OB, a smart woman who seemed also to have a foolish streak, had listened to the heartbeat, like the sound of a rubber band pinging, for about ten seconds before announcing, "This one's a keeper." Then she turned the machine off, looked me in the eye, and said, "OK. We both know anything can happen, but a heartbeat that strong at eight weeks? You're not going to lose this baby."

James's eyes grew wide, just as Kevin's had when I brought home the news. "What kind of a doctor says a thing like that?" I continued. "Especially to an old lady like me?"

James nodded and smiled, taking my hand. "My god," he said, "You're going to have a baby," and there it was again, the parallel world, the sensation of falling, about to hit the water, newly in love.

As the Millay residency drew to a close, my feelings for James were like an emotional flu. I dreamed tender scenes of confession, woke confused and anxious, felt high after talking with him for an hour. When back pain forced him to leave a couple days early, I was bereft. After he'd gone, I burst into tears repeatedly throughout the afternoon and the next day, then spent my penultimate night at the colony listening to the music he'd given me and finishing the bottle of Scotch he'd left behind. On my own last day in paradise, I stayed in bed until 2 p.m., sleeping off a hangover and missing him.

Then the month was done and I was driving west on the New York State Thruway, weeping fiercely. Over the next weeks, as I returned to a full life with Kevin, I checked email obsessively, flushing crimson when a message from James arrived and spending too long composing my responses. "I'm in love," I kept thinking, shaking my head in disbelief and wondering once again what that meant. It's a question that has come up over and over, whenever I've been drawn deeply to someone outside the bounds of pursuit. What does it mean?

I didn't want a romantic future with James, at least not the kind that comes from fulfilling physical desires. But I did want *something*, because being in love is by nature a desirous state. I wanted and wanted, and the wanting, even without a specific outcome, kept me stewing for the rest of that summer. But then summer inched toward fall, and in late September Kevin and I went to New York City for a weekend, and when I saw James, the two of us falling into each other's arms and hugging tightly before separating again, when I introduced him to Kevin and they shook hands, the crush was over. Not right in that moment, not in any moment I could put my finger on, but somewhere in the first part of September, the state of being "in love" had settled into the state of simply loving someone, deeply and permanently. The illness was gone. And the friendship, I knew, would last.

In New York City, the magical afternoon turned into a magical evening, right up until James and I entered the bar where my reading would take place. The crowd was young and uber-hip, and from the moment I ordered a club soda for my complimentary drink, things felt off. And stayed that way. Another reader went on before me, a guy so funny and charming that Chris Rock wouldn't have wanted to follow him, and my reading went over, as my mother used to say, like a fart in church. Afterwards, people flocked to the other guy while I chatted with James and a painter I'd met at a different artist colony months before.

But who cared? Not me, not in my new state. James and the painter and I headed out to dinner at 9:30 p.m., which would have been late on a weeknight in Chicago, but which in New York was perfectly normal. We ate and they drank, and as I watched James and the painter interact, I thought about how not once at any other artist colony had I fallen in love. There had been a little crush on a sculptor once, but it was a surface-level attraction that I suspected would fade if I got to know her. There had been shared meals and liquor and long conversations with many other people in the kind of compressed situation in which I'd met James, in which it is possible to have a discrete affair, and not once had I been tempted. For all my interest in romance, I'm not really a romantic; I approach the mysteries and emotions of love from a rational perspective. I'm not much of a fatalist, either, but admiring James and his now-permanent place in my life made me feel as though our friendship was meant to be.

Soon we were full and it was late and I joked that I needed to get my money's worth out of my exorbitant hotel room. The painter took his leave, and James and I walked to the Union Square subway, which he entered only after I promised to hop immediately into a taxi. I was lying. It was a beautiful night, the air soft and warm, the streets full. I subtracted an hour for Central Time and phoned Kevin, who was watching Letterman's monologue, and said that I'd told James our news. I explained why and he said it made perfect sense, and then I described how happy James was and that he wanted me to pass on congratulations and that I was already at 23rd Street and might as well walk the rest of the way to the hotel.

"I'm sure the air will do you good," Kevin said, not at all concerned about the time or my location or anything, it seemed, even though I knew he felt as nervous as I did about this shared new territory.

We hung up and I kept walking, up Fifth Avenue past the entrance to the Empire State Building, remembering all those teenaged trips into the city with friends looking for some way of enlarging ourselves. We would go to the Metropolitan Museum of Art, the only museum we knew about, and look at images we didn't understand, or walk through Times Square, filled then with prostitutes and peep shows, to shop in a discount clothing store before taking the train north again, feeling we'd survived something. What a different world that was from the street I walked now, so clean and friendly, like the sanitized backdrop of a romantic comedy.

As I walked, playing over the conversation with James and the painter, I felt lucky to be part of the vast web of people who create. Now I was creating physically as well, my body on autopilot, my mind eagerly bounding around. Restless. Inspired. I felt floaty, the way I sometimes had at artist colonies when, after dinner, I returned to my studio believing that anything, anything might happen there.

I'd long understood how important the act of telling was, but that night I felt it deeply, physically. After announcing myself to James, stating my plurality, the effect was subtle but real. I wanted to say it again, loudly, to strangers on the street, to the hotel clerk who glanced up and said "Good evening," to the man in a business suit who shared the elevator to the fifth floor as I fought the urge to twirl around and throw my arms in the air. "I'm pregnant!" I wanted to proclaim out of the blue, a forty-three-year-old woman who, let's be honest, looked every bit her age. What would they think? What would they say in return? "Congratulations," most likely, even if they were thinking, "Are you kidding?"

Opening the door to my room, I was startled by a lamp having been turned on. The bed, which I'd left rumpled after my nap, was smoothed out. The clothes I'd left on it lay folded over the desk chair. The white duvet was turned down, and on the pillow rested a tiny foil plate cupping two dark chocolates. Immediately my mind went into overdrive: How dare they come into my room? I didn't request turndown service! Do they think chocolates justify $650? But right behind those thoughts was a sense of comfort so profound it obliterated everything else. My mother had turned my bed down each night when I was small. Chocolate before bed seemed a grand idea.

It was midnight, but I decided to take advantage of the deep bathtub. I ran a warm bath laced with salts that smelled like a spring forest, and set the foil plate with chocolates on the tub's edge. Soon I was lying back against a perfect slope, water up to my armpits, breasts floating so that they looked young. I popped a chocolate in my mouth, then placed both hands against my abdomen, thumbs and pointer fingers connected in the shape of a heart. I imagined the fetus floating in its saline world, sensing the outer calm, the difference between a bouncy walk along city streets and a quiet bath. My love, I thought. My sky. My life.

I'm having a baby, I said out loud, cringing just slightly at the proclamation but only out of habit. I believed it now, not a hundred percent, not without recognizing the possibility of loss, but more than I'd believed it before. A baby, I said over and over, naming some vague future, some sparkling outcome. I felt in love with the creature floating inside me, the size of a kidney bean, not quite a baby but no longer just a product of my imagination. I felt in love with my life and with all the people in it, including James and especially Kevin, who had agreed that it might be fun to have a child and who was stunned teary by the OB/GYN calling our kid a keeper.

And the hotel room. What a hotel room it was. What a bathtub and what chocolates. What a bed. What a lovely set of windows to wake up beside in the morning, especially if tonight went well and the fetus stayed inside me and continued to grow, and especially if years from now I got to look back on this night as what it felt like then: the beginning of a family.

Who did I think I was? I laughed out loud, popping the second chocolate into my mouth. After all these years, I couldn't answer that question. Or maybe it was just the wrong question. Maybe the better question, asked of every kind of situation, was: who was I on the way to becoming? That was the guiding question of my entire life, and I still didn't have an answer. But the prospect of finding out carried me out of the bath and between the covers in a hotel room that, for the next eight hours, seemed worth every penny.

THE MARRIED KISS

A tremor jostles the bed, his small fist tapping away her dream.

In the dream, she stands in her childhood bedroom in her father's house in Poughkeepsie, New York, suitcase in hand, checking the clock because the train is leaving soon, the plane is leaving soon, it's time to go back home to Chicago, but wait, she's missing something, what's missing? Her mother, she realizes with a start, her mother lives just two miles away, and why hasn't she called her mother? Why hasn't she gone to visit?

This is a recurring theme in the first years after her mother's death, this neglect, this forgetting, and in this particular dream there's still time to remedy the oversight. Cut to the porch of a tall house not far from the Hudson River. The woman runs across it, flinging open the front door and bounding up a flight of stairs. The dreamscape is rich with metaphors she can't pause to decipher: drop cloths covering the steps, thick sheets of plastic hanging on the walls. Regret powers her muscles as she frets that she might be too late, that her mother may no longer live here, but when she reaches the top of the stairs and flings open the door, there stands her mother, smiling in profile. She's a composite of various ages, girlishly slim with salt-and-pepper hair and the glasses of her elder years. In the dim living room, she holds a sheet cake bright with candles, presenting it to a dark-haired adolescent boy. Other people stand in the shadows, the boy's family perhaps, everyone watching as her mother slowly turns her head toward the open door, unsurprised and unimpressed, and nods as if to say, "Come and join us."

The tremor begins just as she steps forward, her mother jostling and fading along with the cake, the strange family, the possibility of reaching out. She wants to hug her mother, to ask how she is, to be recognized and perhaps given a word of solace. Instead, a hand touches her cheek and a voice sings, "Wakey, wakey." Her eyes open to light-brown freckles splattered across his nose, to his sleepy breath entwining with her breath, seeping into her lungs, making her eyelids close again as she floats between the two scenes, the two geographies, the darkness of the living room and the brightness of the bedroom, the world in which she's a daughter and the world in which she's a mother, and which one, she wonders in the momentary, hovering pause, which one is more real?

Impressionism. Like realism but with shorter brush-strokes, thicker paint, lines that don't distinguish so much as meld. If realism is a photograph, impressionism is the view through eyelashes, a reminder that someone mulled over this scene, made decisions about light and color, embraced the imperfections and loose approximations of the subjective.

In Mary Cassatt's *Breakfast in Bed*, a child, toddler-age, sits upright against a mother, her arm encircling his waist in secure intimacy. Soft colors cohere across the fuzzy borders of their bodies: the white teacup on the side table blurs into the white plate beneath it, into the white pillow and sheets, the white sleeves of the reclining mother's nightgown, the child's white shirt, all the whites laced with subtle gray-blues that migrate into ruddy cheeks, into the mother's arms and child's fleshy hands and legs, their bodies defined by the curve of faint shadows.

Mary Cassatt wasn't a mother. Or a wife, knowing as she did that marriage would curtail her life as an artist. She was a daughter, sister, sister-in-law, aunt. And a leading impressionist painter, her reputation already formed by the time she began making the scenes for which she's now best known: mothers and young children engaged in everyday acts. Nursing, bathing, kissing, waking. In "Breakfast in Bed," the mother lounges, looking past her child with an unfocused gaze, her thoughts on the day ahead, perhaps, or on the dream world she so recently left. The child's chubby hand clutches a biscuit, eyes fixed on an object beyond the frame, something whose allure might shortly cause it to squirm against the mother's embrace. The painting captures a still moment before the breaking away, the leaping from bed into the accumulation of push-and-pull days.

"Wakey, my beloved," the boy whispers, such improbable wording in such a high-pitched voice. Four years old and counting.

She'd started calling him "my beloved" during the newborn phase, when she rocked from bedroom to living room to kitchen and back, thinking of Toni Morrison's novel, of a mother's desperate choice to extinguish her child, of history's horrors: slave auctions, kinder transports, the Trail of Tears. How, she wondered, has the human race survived its own cruelty?

She was tired. By three months old, the baby slept decently at night, but that hardly mattered. She was tired of his relentless need. She wanted time to herself. She wanted to take a nap, read a book in the bathtub, become a person she recognized again. Not a mother. Not just a mother.

"My beloved," she cooed, holding the baby against her chest, patting his back and jouncing, bedroom to dining room to living room and back again. It was a performance, a conscious effort to behave the way a parent should. Her own mother had loved her fiercely, joyfully, and then less joyfully when she was old enough to hold opinions and disagree, but as a baby the woman had been loved without question, and the solid, unshakable certainty of that beginning had carried her through the decades. So she held her own baby, rubbed his back, whispered "my beloved" even though what she felt toward him was commitment, devotion, investment in the boy he would one day become and in the family they already were, but not love. She did not love her baby.

Like the view through eyelashes, the sound from underwater. Amygdala. Ah-MIG-duh-luh. Meaning almond-like in Greek because that's the shape of it, of them, sitting under the cauliflower folds of the temporal lobes, behind the eye sockets and in line with the ears, twin centers that function as one. Receiving impressions, making responses, creating memory to protect us from danger. Or in the case of a new mother, enlarging until she becomes hyper-attentive to the baby's needs, even anxious and obsessive about them.

The woman assumed her amygdala grew as it was supposed to because, in one recurring dream from the first year of motherhood, she and the baby's father were on their way back from a movie when she realized they'd left the baby home alone. Again the neglect, again the for-getting, the shock of remembering. She urged the baby's father to drive faster, hurry, hurry, the image of the baby crying with no one to answer making her hyperventilate. When she woke from those dreams, emotion hummed through her brain and torso, so realistic it was hard to believe she hadn't yet abandoned the child.

There were also brief moments of euphoria, courtesy of the amygdala, when she focused on the baby's beauty, on his round face and long eyelashes resting against translu-cent skin, on the weight of him in her arm and the connec-tion he offered to the long line of human begetting. She felt an intense sense of rightness then, but the romance of new motherhood, the heart-pounding love, the goofy smiles and contentment she'd witnessed in friends, didn't materialize. She hadn't fallen in love with the baby, didn't feel he was really hers. He was a curiosity, a guest come to visit from another realm, someone who might yet decide to move along in search of a better home.

Not loving him wasn't a source of sadness. It didn't fill her with guilt or a sense of failure. The presence of love wasn't something she could control. It would arrive even-tually, she thought, and in the meantime, she vowed to be honest, to remain open and patient but not forceful, espe-cially since her strongest emotion some days was confu-sion over how babies, with their unformed personalities and lack of appreciation, could inspire all the love we're expected to feel.

"Wakey, wakey," the boy calls. She lies very still, eyes closed, waiting for the next step in their ritual, his thumb and forefinger pinching together and carefully prying her eyelid open as his voice whispers louder, determined to seduce her back from the dream world, "Mama, come be with me."

It's risky for a mother to admit she doesn't feel what's expected of her. Ayelet Waldman learned this after publishing a "Modern Love" column in the *New York Times* in which she explained that, unlike most of her mother-friends, she had a terrific sex life, perhaps because she loved her husband more than their four children. Waldman didn't say she *didn't* love the kids, just that she loved the husband more, and enraged messages flooded her inbox. *The View* co-host Star Jones railed against her on air. Oprah Winfrey devoted a whole show to exploring the scandal. A mother is supposed to put her children first, sacrifice everything and subordinate herself to their needs, love them more than she loves anyone else. And, the assumption goes, this love should begin at the moment of birth, if not before, or the woman's a monster.

Relax the eyes. Squint. Look at Medea, the most famous example of a monstrous mother, a woman who killed her two sons as revenge against their father abandoning her for another woman. But even Medea loved her children, as Euripedes makes clear. She knew that losing them would turn her mad with grief, but she was already mad with a different kind of grief and calculated that the pain of losing her children would be less than the pain of allowing their father's mistreatment of her to go unpunished. She loved him more than she loved them, or maybe she hated him more than she loved them, or maybe to Medea that was the same thing.

The woman's own mother had once loved her kids more than anyone else. It was her father who took revenge, filing for custody on the grounds of a monstrous relationship. Her mother tried to call his bluff, but when he didn't back down and the court date was scheduled, she caved. Reconciled. Moved back "home." Sank into a depression that made clear the mistake: she loved the kids with all her heart but not more, no longer more, than anyone else in the world. Months later, when she left again, the daughter stayed behind because someone had to, and her mother accepted that trade-off. Freedom for a child. Who was strong-willed anyway, independent, would be OK on her own, her mother must have thought. And she was, although the leaving stayed with her the way leaving often does, a wound scabbing over as its importance grows with time.

When the baby was four months old, the new family moved to Spain for a season. Each day, strangers stopped them on the streets of Madrid to tug on the baby's toes, kiss his hands. "He's so beautiful," they said, touching his mini cargo pants and chunky sweaters, marveling at the American way of dressing infants like teenagers. Then, just before Christmas, when the baby was eight months old, they moved back to Chicago, and two weeks later, on New Year's Day, the woman's mother died.

The shock was electric, recurrent, zipping down her spine and out to her fingertips, making her mind go blank hour after hour, day after day. The only thing that brought her out of that state was the baby. In the cloudy time before and after the funeral, as she sorted through boxes of papers in a Las Vegas mobile home while the baby tried to crawl across the carpeted floor, she felt an appreciation so deep she mistook it for love. How lucky she was to have him, how unbearable life would have been without his needs and demands, his drooling smiles. But weeks later, back home again, with grief settling into the fabric of her days, she discovered that gratitude is gratitude, no more, no less. "Do I *love* him?" she asked herself once again, and the answer seemed murky at best. What, she wondered, would love for a child—real, deep, unconditional love—feel like?

It was hard to tell then what story she was living, what narrative through-line might guide her back to a life she recognized. Some days she felt estranged, permanently, from herself, and other days she felt close to insight, to some revelation of how the various plot points lined up.

Things began to change when the baby learned to pull himself to a standing position and shuffle around while hanging onto the couch, the coffee table, the window-sill. "Cruising," it's called. Although the woman and the baby's father were constantly on guard now for what he might pull on top of him, although they were exhausted from holding the tiny hands and walking him around the apartment, bent backs aching, something shifted inside her. Now, when the baby bumped his head or fell down hard and began to cry, he turned toward her, hands reaching for comfort, and she saw the upside of the whole endeavor. Felt the release of endorphins. The Pavlovian comfort in a face pressed to her chest, fingers holding onto her ear as he cried.

But it wasn't until a couple weeks before the boy's first birthday that her amygdala went into overdrive. That's when the tantrum stage began, the terrible two's having arrived a full year early, when everything provoked a crisis, from the color of a plastic cup to the number of toys in a bath. Even the gentlest rebuke—"Honey, we don't pull the kitty's tail because it hurts her"—made the boy fall to the floor, kicking and throwing an arm over his eyes, wailing like a thespian. Receiving no response, he would go silent for a moment, lift the arm and check his audience before wailing some more. Standing above him the woman felt dizzy, exhilarated, her heart beating wildly and eyes filling with ecstatic tears. Here was a boy who bypassed disappointment and went straight to fury at the injustices of life, the impossibility of moving through time unscathed. Here was a personality emerging from the carapace of infancy, guns blazing. She envied him, admired him, adored him, loved him.

Cassatt's mothers love their babies. You can see it in the tender bend of their necks, in the cheeks pressed to the tops of small heads, in their eyes, so patient and engaged. But do the babies love their mothers? That depends, perhaps, on who stands before the images. And on how we understand the contours of love.

For a long time the woman tried to nail love down, searching literature and philosophy and science for clues about how we define it. Then, in the early stage of her father's dying, a nurse in the hospital asked him to rate his pain on a scale of one to ten. He took a long time to answer, testing the weight of each number against the failures of his body, until his daughter couldn't stand the silence. "Ten would be the most pain you've ever felt," she said, and the nurse corrected her: "The scale is whatever he says it is. Believe me, some patients never go above a five and others call a hangnail a twelve." The pain scale has meaning only in relation to the patient's own perceptions.

After that, the woman began to think of love as similar to pain. Impossible to define objectively. Understandable only to the person who feels it, who weighs it against memories. She remembered how a friend once insisted that the woman *did* love her baby, of course she did, she just didn't *call* it love. "And he loves you, too," the friend said, nearly angry, and the woman nodded, pretending to consider those words. But that wasn't how she understood her own story.

During the toddler years, the woman and the boy's father often went together to pick him up from daycare. When the boy saw them, his face transformed from concentration to joy, and he dropped whatever truck or car he'd been maneuvering and kick-stepped toward them. When she bent to receive him, opening her arms wide, he'd duck around her and fall against his father's knees, hugging tight before stretching his hands upward.

"I am so sorry," the teacher's assistant said more than once, hand on her heart. "He must be going through a phase."

But the woman knew it wasn't a phase, or rather, she knew that this phase had been in place from the start. The boy loved his father more, and why not? His father was a lovable man, a cheerful, laid-back, funny presence, and he spent more time with the boy than she did. One night a week she taught a graduate class, which meant she dropped the boy off in the morning and didn't see him awake again until the following morning. She thought of those 24-hour periods as vacations, times when she could return to the freedoms of her old life, grabbing an early dinner out, taking the train home at 10 p.m. She enjoyed being away long enough to miss him and then returning home, tiptoeing into the boy's room, watching for subtle movements in his slumbering cheeks. The price for enjoying time without him was that he didn't favor her, and she could accept that. It seemed a fair exchange.

Then one afternoon when the boy was two-and-a-half, his father picked him up from daycare while she stayed behind, grading. When they arrived home, the boy came up the building's interior stairs, gripping the spindles and grunting with the effort of reaching the apartment's front door, where she stood waiting. His expression was tired and proud, brown eyes glistening, nose red from the end of a cold, and she scooped him up, kissed him, told him what a good job he'd done climbing. She carried him to an armchair and sat down, asking about his day. Was school fun? Did Sebastian try to bite him again?

The boy answered in monosyllables, yes, no, then turned to face her, straddling her legs, a foot tucked alongside each of her hips. Outside the window, maple branches swung lush and shadowy, and a Lake Michigan breeze came through the balcony's screen door. They sat still, breathing in sync, listening to his father opening and closing cabinets in the kitchen as he started dinner. It was a scene Mary Cassatt would have painted beautifully, attention on the mother's face, contentment on the child's, a moment of calm union in the midst of the everyday.

The boy began to smile, foolishly at first and then with great tenderness. He scootched a little closer, pressed a palm to her cheek, raised his eyebrows as he peered into her eyes and reached the other hand to her forehead, carefully pushing back her hair. Using both hands he opened the top of her blouse and leaned forward to kiss her skin. He smiled again, a lopsided little grin she'd seen on other faces, at other points in her life, and said, "I love you, Mama."

Just then his father walked into the living room, and the Oedipal stage, which she hadn't believed in before that moment, began. "Do you want corn tortillas or flour tortillas?" the boy's father asked her, and a cloud descended, wrinkling the boy's forehead, pursing his lips. A new voice, deep and guttural, rumbled up from his belly and turned in the direction of the man who was now, suddenly, his rival. "Go away, Daddy," the voice growled, strong and adamant. "Daddy, you go *away.*"

Whites and blues, deep pinks and tans, the browns and reds of cheeks, of bodies connected across time and space, all the way back to the classical world in which Queen Jocasta doesn't appear to have loved her baby, or even felt committed to him, at least not during his infancy. Even before Oedipus was conceived, King Laius had been warned that his son would one day kill him and marry the queen, so after the baby arrived, Jocasta carried him to a nearby hillside, lay him in the sun, and walked away, intending to subvert the prophecy. But fate, of course, weaves every possibility into its tapestry. A shepherd soon found the boy, and Oedipus grew into a strapping young man who did everything he was destined to do.

Oedipus the King loved Queen Jocasta and, Sophocles tells us, governed equally with her for many years. For her part, Jocasta loved Oedipus the man so much that, upon realizing his true identity, she hung herself. Sophocles doesn't blame her, any more than he blames Oedipus for in turn gouging out his eyes and exiling himself from the kingdom. Both Oedipus and Jocasta, playthings of the gods, behave as they must, offering reasonable responses to an impossible situation.

Still. It's hard not to think about the events Sophocles doesn't dramatize. Jocasta carrying the baby out of the palace and through the streets to a path leading slowly up into the hills. The solid weight of the baby in her arms, the brushing of grass against her ankles. Does she rock him, pat his back and coo into his ear, soothe him to make the trip more bearable? When she arrives on the hillside, at an open place exposed to the heat of the sun, to insects and animals, does she sink down to her knees before laying him on the ground? What if Mary Cassatt had painted that moment, the steely tenderness just before abandonment? Imagine the colors, the orange and tan of dry earth, the unblemished blue of sky and eyes, the fuzzy union of skin, cloth, dirt, the shadows cast by betrayal.

"Mama, come *on*," he whispers in the first light of day, eyes frustrated but mouth still ready to grin. "It's time to play."

She pulls her head back, twisting away from the fingers opening her eye, and lifts the covers. He crawls in, syncing his body to hers, one arm slung across her neck. She asks if he had a good sleep, and he nods. "I've been thinking about the setup we can make," he says. She knows they should get up because it's Sunday and there's no point in waking his father, too, at—what time is it?—6:14 a.m., but the bed is warm, his body is warm.

His father. At the beginning of the boy's life, the woman understood Ayelet Waldman's point. There was so much pressure to mother well, so much expectation that the baby would become the center of her world, but the man was at the center, enduring the difficult newborn days along with her. She couldn't imagine doing it without him.

Later, though, they both became conscious of how they'd stopped casually touching each other throughout the day, no longer running a hand over a back or slinging limbs over one another on the couch, because they touched the boy constantly, their tactile needs met and exceeded every hour by his physicality. They agreed to correct this shift, making a conscious effort not only to stay connected but to show their son that his parents love each other, to model for him what neither of them had experienced in childhood.

The boy whispers about the setup, about the tiny men he'll position on horseback outside a castle, poised for battle. He loves to make a world and control every aspect of it, and she loves that he loves this. Sometimes she photographs the setup, then types the story he narrates about it, and they paste everything into a construction-paper book that he thumbs through at bedtime.

As he talks, she runs a hand down his smooth back, over a butt cheek that fits perfectly in her palm, to the muscle of his outer thigh. He scootches closer, pressing his chest and cheek to hers, elbow resting on her shoulder as his fingers reach into her hair and rub so lightly her eyes flutter closed. Time shifts and there's a brief sensation of falling before she opens her eyes again. She has been here before, so many times, with young men and older men, with the boy's father, and this is not that, of course it's not that, but then again, in some measure, it is also that. The delight of bodies, the way the amygdala lights up in similar ways for romantic love and maternal love, the senses feeding signals to the almonds in the early morning light, then and now, him and me and her and the pain of absence, always present, the permanent imprint, the taste, the gentle lip-smacking mmmm-ma, mmmm-ma, ma, ma, mama.

In *Mother's Kiss*, Cassatt shows the influence of Japanese printmaking. A mother sits on a chair, cradling a naked toddler, their bodies created by simple lines. The child's fleshy legs bend around the mother's arm, its hips angle toward her chest, its neck rests in the crook of her arm. The child's visible hand grasps the collar of the mother's dress, while the mother's hands press against its back and butt. Her head bends toward the child's face, their lips just beginning to touch, her eyes closed or nearly so, and the child's eyes open and cast to the side, perhaps remembering some denial or sadness. The child is innocent (naked), vulnerable (sad-eyed), receiving comfort (the kiss). But the mother's stance, the bent arm, bent neck, the way the crook of her elbow brings the small head forward for the kiss, is also romantic. Enveloping, communicative, not just meeting a need but displaying a need to express a depth of feeling that infuses every bone and muscle. Cassatt understood something about motherhood that many mothers deny.

Sometimes when she puts the boy to bed in the evening, when she's home and it's her turn, he does exactly what she did as a child. Begs her not to leave. Invents new questions, new reasons why she must return to him, again and again. "Wait, wait, Mama. No, listen. Really." He giggles, hardly able to say the words, aware of what he's doing and unable to stop. And just as her mother did, she indulges him longer than she should, until frustration creeps into her voice and then anger. But before that, sometimes she lies beside him for a while, rubbing as he talks, his speech growing drowsy, her hand going up and down his body, soothing, appreciating, imagining the man he'll become.

"Sometimes he presents his body to me/like a present he knows I want / but will not take," writes Sheryl St. Germain in her gorgeous poem, "My Son's Body":

. . . how could I not understand

wanting to have it, to touch it
not as a mother but as the beloved
how could I not understand
thinking to enter into that beauty,
forgetting the way possession
turns everything it wants
into itself.

The story goes like this: Once the woman had a baby and did not love him, and now she has a boy, four years old and five and six, whom she adores and who returns her love so vehemently that sometimes when she gets back from a trip—to a conference or an artist colony or a foreign country—he lashes out. Pokes her cheek hard with his index finger. Drives a truck into her ankle. Gives a kick as she walks by. She and his father put him in time-out when this happens, his eyes wet with injustice, and later, at bedtime, she and the boy lie in his dim room and she asks why he hurts her. The boy frowns. Shrugs. Thinks for a moment. Says, "Mama, I just love you too much."

She believes him. He loves her too much, as we all do, from time to time, love someone too much, the excess of emotion a pleasure and a wound. Betrayal is woven into the fabric of relationships, into the negotiation between subject and object, self and other, lover and beloved, but miraculously, even the worst betrayals aren't always deal-breakers. Jocasta left Oedipus on the hillside and later hung herself, yes, but in between there were years of happiness, years of Oedipus the King loving her unfathomably. The woman's own mother left her, broke up with her in a way, but they came together again, however imperfectly. Maybe, she thinks, a limited, intense period of all-consuming love is as much a gift as any of us can hope for.

She kisses the boy's forehead. It's late, he has to sleep, there is school in the morning, she says. She doesn't say that she's looking forward to going downstairs and sitting on the couch with the boy's father, the man who takes so much in stride. She wants to talk with him about the day, laughing and yawning the way they do each night, all these years into the best, most stable relationship of her life.

But the boy shakes off his drowsiness and scrambles from under the covers. "Mama, wait. Mama, just one thing, I promise. One last thing. Please. Just this."

How long the days are, and how short the years. She steps back to the bed on which he stands now, beckoning her, and time turns inside out until she's standing in his place, raising her arms up, hearing her voice in his: "Come closer." She wants to hug her own mother, press her face into the familiar neck, feel the reassurance of loving arms that will never leave her, of life stretching forward, world without end, amen.

Her son does not hug her. Instead he grasps her shoulders, a lopsided smile on his face, and suppresses a giggle. "OK, Mama," he says. "Let's practice."

"Practice what?"

"The kiss," he says, squaring his shoulders and taking a breath. His hands move to her face, palms gently cup her cheeks, and she is no longer him, reaching toward her own mother, but herself standing in his room, receiving the kind of kiss he's seen at the end of movies, when the prince and princess finally unite. "The married kiss," he'll call it later, the one that means you really love someone. His lips touch hers, gently at first and then pressing, fingers holding her face, legs planted and upper body taut, the future opening up before him and closing down before her but not yet, not quite yet, and she feels enveloped, feels the through-line of wanting and being wanted, the heart-pounding story that doesn't at all apply, yet here it is, again and again, here is romantic love showing up unprompted and unannounced, provocative and powerful, silly and sublime.

She opens her eyes wide, wondering what to do, what to say, how to navigate this new terrain, but of course there are no answers, there are only questions dissolving into more questions. So she does the only thing that makes sense: she closes her eyes again and waits, allowing herself to feel the presence, the ever-presence of romance in all its many forms, most of which are puzzles, mysteries that point us toward deep reflection on who we are and how we live. *Remember this,* she thinks, holding very still, filled with awe, the boy's warm lips still pressed against her own.

ACKNOWLEDGMENTS

Editors of literary journals do tireless, essential work, and I'm grateful to several who published early chapters of this book, sometimes in very different form: Evelyn Sommers, *Missouri Review* ("About Wayne"), Dinty Moore, *Brevity* ("Backstitch"), Heide Wiedner, *Under the Sun* ("Boy Crazy"), Philip Graham, *Ninth Letter* ("Crushed"), Barrie Jean Borich, *Water~Stone Review* ("Evenings at the Collegeview Diner"), and Steve Church, *The Normal School* ("How to Tell a True Love Story"). Thanks also to Marcia Aldrich for including "Breaking and Entering" in her anthology *WaveForm: Twenty-First Century Essays by Women* (University of Georgia Press, 2016). I'm indebted to the generosity of Sheryl St. Germain, who gave me not only her beautiful poetry collection, *The Journals of Scheherazade* (University of North Texas, 1996), but also permission to reprint lines from "My Son's Body."

Kristen Elias Rowley and the team at The Ohio State University Press produce consistently gorgeous books, and I'm grateful to be part of the family. Many thanks to my wonderful publicist Sheryl Johnston.

Thank you to my colleagues at DePaul University for their generosity, wisdom, and inspiration, including Miles Harvey who gave me Calvino's "Chloe" and Gioia Diliberto, who encouraged me to think about romantic friendships. The DePaul Humanities Center, College of Liberal Arts and Social Sciences, and University Research Council offered time and financial support for writing. Research assistant Borja Cabada provided expert help. I'm grateful to the Illinois Arts Council and to Ragdale, where portions of this book were drafted.

Writer and mentor extraordinaire Carl Klaus offered generous feedback on the manuscript. Jessica Peri Chalmers, Sarah Dohrmann, Mary Hawley, Susan Joy, Vesna Neskow, Lee Reilly, Rima Rantisi, and Maija Rothenberg helped move the project toward completion. Heartfelt appreciation to Chris Green and cin salach, whose Tiger Room Salon provides literary sustenance and a warm audience for work in progress.

Tim Hillegonds talked me through a good deal of this manuscript, designed my website, and once caught me mid-faint at 7,000 feet. I'm grateful for his friendship, wisdom, and reflexes.

Francesca Royster was the first reader for some of these essays, and her generous spirit, grace, and tenacity always help me write. My work also benefits from Rebecca Soglin's steadfast friendship, appreciation for the absurd, solid ethical center, and welcoming home.

James Cañón's willingness to bet a thousand dollars spurred me to complete a first draft of this book, and his friendship inspires, motivates, and entertains me every day. *Mil gracias.*

Thank you to Mike Morano, who gave me his blessing to tell the stories of our family as I remember them, and to Monica Schott, the sister I never had.

It's the great fortune of my life to be the mother of Andrew Quirk, who was patient during much of my writing time and hilariously distracting during the rest. To Kevin Quirk, who literally feeds me and who offers time, space, peace of mind, and partnership in crafting this crazy, beautiful, ever-romantic existence, *thank you.*

MACHETE
Joy Castro, Series Editor

This series showcases fresh stories, innovative forms, and books that break new aesthetic ground in nonfiction—memoir, personal and lyric essay, literary journalism, cultural meditations, short shorts, hybrid essays, graphic pieces, and more—from authors whose writing has historically been marginalized, ignored, and passed over. The series is explicitly interested in not only ethnic and racial diversity, but also gender and sexual diversity, neurodiversity, physical diversity, religious diversity, cultural diversity, and diversity in all of its manifestations. The machete enables path-clearing; it hacks new trails and carves out new directions. The Machete series celebrates and shepherds unique new voices into publication, providing a platform for writers whose work intervenes in dangerous ways.